بسم الله الرحمن الرحيم

About The Author

The author, who writes under the pen-name HARUN YAHYA, was born in Ankara in 1956. Having completed his primary and secondary education in Ankara, he then studied arts at Istanbul's Mimar Sinan University and philosophy at Istanbul University. Since the 1980s, the author has published many books on political, faith-related and scientific issues. Harun Yahya is well-known as an author who has written very important works disclosing the imposture of evolutionists, the invalidity of their claims and the dark liaisons between Darwinism and bloody ideologies.

His pen-name is made up of the names "Harun" (Aaron) and "Yahya" (John), in memory of the two esteemed prophets who fought against lack of faith. The Prophet's seal on the cover of the author's books has a symbolic meaning linked to the their contents. This seal represents the Qur'an as the last Book by God and the last word of Him and our Prophet, the last of all the prophets. Under the guidance of the Qur'an and Sunnah, the author makes it his main goal to disprove each one of the fundamental tenets of godless ideologies and to have the "last word", so as to completely silence the objections raised against religion. The seal of the Prophet, who attained ultimate wisdom and moral perfection, is used as a sign of his intention of saying this last word.

All these works by the author centre around one goal: to convey the message of the Qur'an to people, thus encouraging them to think about basic faith-related issues, such as the existence of God, His unity and the hereafter, and to display the decrepit foundations and perverted works of godless systems. Harun Yahya enjoys a wide readership in many countries, from India to America, England to Indonesia, Poland to Bosnia, and Spain to Brazil. Some of his books are available in English, French, German, Italian, Portuguese, Urdu, Arabic, Albanian, Russian, Serbo-Croat (Bosnian), Uygur Turkish, and Indonesian, and they have been enjoyed by readers all over the world.

Greatly appreciated all around the world, these works have been instrumental in many people putting their faith in God and in many others gaining a deeper insight into their faith. The wisdom, and the sincere and easy-to-understand style employed give these books a distinct touch which directly strikes any one who reads or examines them. Immune to objections, these works are characterised by their features of rapid effectiveness, definite results and irrefutability. It is unlikely that those who read these books and give a serious thought to them can any longer sincerely advocate the materialistic philosophy, atheism and any other perverted ideology or philosophy. Even if they continue to advocate, this will be only a sentimental insistence since these books have refuted these ideologies from their very basis. All contemporary movements of denial are ideologically defeated today, thanks to the collection of books written by Harun Yahya.

There is no doubt that these features result from the wisdom and lucidity of the Qur'an. The author certainly does not feel proud of himself; he merely intends to serve as a means in one's search for God's right path. Furthermore, no material gain is sought in the publication of these works.

Considering these facts, those who encourage people to read these books, which open the "eyes" of the heart and guide them in becoming more devoted servants of God, render an invaluable service.

Meanwhile, it would just be a waste of time and energy to propagate books which create confusion in peoples' minds, lead man into ideological chaos, and which, clearly have no strong and precise effects in removing the doubts in peoples' hearts, as also verified from previous experience. It is apparent that it is impossible for books devised to emphasize the author's literary power rather than the noble goal of saving people from loss of faith, to have such a great effect. Those who doubt this can readily see that the sole aim of Harun Yahya's books is to overcome disbelief and to disseminate the moral values of the Qur'an. The success, impact and sincerity this service has attained are manifest in the reader's conviction.

One point needs to be kept in mind: The main reason for the continuing cruelty and conflict, and all the ordeals Muslims undergo is the ideological prevalence of disbelief. These things can only come to an end with the ideological defeat of disbelief and by ensuring that everybody knows about the wonders of creation and Qur'anic morality, so that people can live by it. Considering the state of the world today, which forces people into the downward spiral of violence, corruption and conflict, it is clear that this service has to be provided more speedily and effectively. Otherwise, it may be too late.

It is no exaggeration to say that the collection of books by Harun Yahya have assumed this leading role. By the Will of God, these books will be the means through which people in the 21st century will attain the peace and bliss, justice and happiness promised in the Qur'an.

The works of the author include *The New Masonic Order, Judaism and Freemasonry, The Disasters Darwinism Brought to Humanity, Communism in Ambush, The Bloody Ideology of Darwinism: Fascism, The 'Secret Hand' in Bosnia, Behind the Scenes of The Holocaust, Behind the Scenes of Terrorism, Israel's Kurdish Card, Solution: The Morals of the Qur'an, Articles 1-2-3, A Weapon of Satan: Romantism, Truths 1-2, The Western World Turns to God, The Evolution Deceit, Precise Answers to Evolutionists, Evolutionary Falsehoods, Perished Nations, For Men of Understanding, The Prophet Moses, The Prophet Joseph, The Golden Age, Allah's Artistry in Colour, Glory is Everywhere, The Truth of the Life of This World, Knowing the Truth, Eternity Has Already Begun, Timelessness and the Reality of Fate, The Dark Magic of Darwinism, The Religion of Darwinism, The Collapse of the Theory of Evolution in 20 Questions, Allah is Known Through Reason, The Qur'an Leads the Way to Science, The Real Origin of Life, Consciousness in the Cell, A String of Miracles, The Creation of the*

Universe, Miracles of the Qur'an, The Design in Nature, Self-Sacrifice and Intelligent Behaviour Models in Animals, The End of Darwinism, Deep Thinking, Never Plead Ignorance, The Green Miracle Photosynthesis, The Miracle in the Cell, The Miracle in the Eye, The Miracle in the Spider, The Miracle in the Gnat, The Miracle in the Ant, The Miracle of the Immune System, The Miracle of Creation in Plants, The Miracle in the Atom, The Miracle in the Honeybee, The Miracle of Seed, The Miracle of Hormone, The Miracle of the Termite, The Miracle of the Human Being, The Miracle of Man's Creation, The Miracle of Protein, The Secrets of DNA.

The author's childrens books are: *Children Darwin Was Lying!*, *The World of Animals*, *The Splendour in the Skies*, *The World of Our Little Friends: The Ants*, *Honeybees That Build Perfect Combs*, *Skillful Dam Builders: Beavers*.

The author's other works on Quranic topics include: *The Basic Concepts in the Qur'an, The Moral Values of the Qur'an, Quick Grasp of Faith 1-2-3, Ever Thought About the Truth?, Crude Understanding of Disbelief, Devoted to Allah, Abandoning the Society of Ignorance, The Real Home of Believers: Paradise, Knowledge of the Qur'an, Qur'an Index, Emigrating for the Cause of Allah, The Character of the Hypocrite in the Qur'an, The Secrets of the Hypocrite, The Names of Allah, Communicating the Message and Disputing in the Qur'an, Answers from the Qur'an, Death Resurrection Hell, The Struggle of the Messengers, The Avowed Enemy of Man: Satan, The Greatest Slander: Idolatry, The Religion of the Ignorant, The Arrogance of Satan, Prayer in the Qur'an, The Importance of Conscience in the Qur'an, The Day of Resurrection, Never Forget, Disregarded Judgements of the Qur'an, Human Characters in the Society of Ignorance, The Importance of Patience in the Qur'an, General Information from the Qur'an, The Mature Faith, Before You Regret, Our Messengers Say, The Mercy of Believers, The Fear of Allah, The Nightmare of Disbelief, Jesus Will Return, Beauties Presented by the Qur'an for Life, A Bouquet of the Beauties of Allah 1-2-3-4, The Iniquity Called "Mockery", The Mystery of the Test, The True Wisdom According to the Qur'an, The Struggle with the Religion of Irreligion, The School of Yusuf, The Alliance of the Good, Slanders Spread Against Muslims Throughout History, The Importance of Following the Good Word, Why Do You Deceive Yourself?, Islam: The Religion of Ease, Enthusiasm and Excitement in the Qur'an, Seeing Good in Everything, How do the Unwise Interpret the Qur'an?, Some Secrets of the Qur'an, The Courage of Believers, Being Hopeful in the Qur'an, Justice and Tolerance in the Qur'an, Basic Tenets of Islam, Those Who do not Listen to the Qur'an.*

TO THE READER

The reason why a special chapter is assigned to the collapse of the theory of evolution is that this theory constitutes the basis of all anti-spiritual philosophies. Since Darwinism rejects the fact of creation, and therefore the existence of God, during the last 140 years it has caused many people to abandon their faith or fall into doubt. Therefore, showing that this theory is a deception is a very important duty, which is strongly related to the religion (deen). It is imperative that this important service be rendered to everyone. Some of our readers may find the chance to read only one of our books. Therefore, we think it appropriate to spare a chapter for a summary of this subject.

In all the books by the author, faith-related issues are explained in the light of the Qur'anic verses and people are invited to learn God's words and to live by them. All the subjects that concern God's verses are explained in such a way as to leave no room for doubt or question marks in the reader's mind. The sincere, plain and fluent style employed ensures that everyone of every age and from every social group can easily understand the books. This effective and lucid narrative makes it possible to read them in a single sitting. Even those who rigorously reject spirituality are influenced by the facts recounted in these books and cannot refute the truthfulness of their contents.

This book and all the other works of the author can be read individually or discussed in a group at a time of conversation. Those readers who are willing to profit from the books will find discussion very useful in the sense that they will be able to relate their own reflections and experiences to one another.
In addition, it will be a great service to the religion to contribute to the presentation and reading of these books, which are written solely for the good pleasure of God. All the books of the author are extremely convincing. For this reason, for those who want to communicate the religion to other people, one of the most effective methods is to encourage them to read these books.

It is hoped that the reader will take time to look through the review of other books on the final pages of the book, and appreciate the rich source of material on faith-related issues, which are very useful and a pleasure to read.

In these books, you will not find, as in some other books, the personal views of the author, explanations based on dubious sources, styles that are unobservant of the respect and reverence due to sacred subjects, nor hopeless, doubt-creating, and pessimistic accounts that create deviations in the heart.

THE ALLIANCE OF THE GOOD

AGAINST THE MORAL DEGRADATION CAUSED BY LACK OF FAITH

*Those who disbelieve are the friends
and protectors of one another. If you do not act in
this way (protect each other), there will be
turmoil in the land and great corruption.
(Surat al-Anfal: 73)*

HARUN YAHYA

January, 2002

THE ALLIANCE OF THE GOOD

HARUN YAHYA

Edited by: David Livingstone

ISBN No.: 81-7231-372-1

Edition: 2002

Published by Abdul Naeem for
Islamic Book Service
2241, Kucha Chelan, Darya Ganj,New Delhi - 110 002 (INDIA)
Ph.: 3253514, 3265380, 3286551,Fax: 3277913
e-mail: ibsdelhi@del2.vsnl.net.in & ibsdelhi@mantraonline.com
website: http://www.islamic-india.com

OUR ASSOCIATES

Islamic Book Service Inc.
136, Charlotte Ave, Hicksville,N. Y. 11801,U.S.A.,
Tel.: 8700-427, Toll Free: 8662424135

Al Munna Book Shop Ltd.
P.O. Box-3449, Sharjah (U.A.E.), Tel.: 06-561-5483, 06-561-4650
Branch: Dubai, Tel.: 04-43529294

Zainab Foundation
Al-Baraka House,18-20, Park Street, Slough, Berkshire,
SLI IPD, England, Tel.: 533-511

Sartaj Company
P.O. Box-48535, Qualbert-4078,South Africa, Tel.: 305-3025

Printed at:
Noida Printing Press,C-31, Sector 7, Noida (U.P.),Ph.: 91-4528211

All translations from the Qur'an are from "The Noble Qur'an: a New Rendering of its Meaning in English"
by Hajj Abdalhaqq and Aisha Bewley, published by Bookwork, Norwich, UK. 1420 CE/1999 AH.

Website: http: // www.harunyahya.com
E-mail: info@harunyahya.com

CONTENTS

INTRODUCTION

As you watch television, read the newspaper, or pass by somewhere, you run into many issues which you would rather not hear about or see. People abandoned to hunger, murders, massacres, the oppressed unable to stand up for their rights, discord, curses, insulting and demeaning language, and general unrest, for which the blame can be attributed to conflicts of interests, and tyrannies and so on...

There is no doubt that you, like everyone else, would like to live in a society where people are committed to peace and security, where people hesitate to oppress or harm one another, and always hear good, loving, caring, and honoring words from one another. Such an environment, ensuring a structure of relationships shaped by respect and love, is everyone's dream. As you flip through channels on television, turn the pages of a newspaper, at home or at your workplace, you would love to see happy, joyful, friendly, sincere, honest, respectful people of good nature displaying moral perfection. Surely, you would like to hear nothing but good news.

However, hoping that one day things will spontaneously change for the better would only be wishful thinking. Therefore, those who are sincerely willing to live in a society where peace, security and freedom prevail, should waste no time in taking action and be willing to make certain sacrifices.

Once you carefully evaluate events unfolding around with intelligence, conscience and common sense, you will recognize the existence of people who are whole-heartedly committed to establishing all the values of goodness mentioned above, and who devote all their time, resources and energy to this cause. While these people, wholly devoted to an all-out effort to make righteousness and good prevail, are exposed to unfair treatment from time to time, or intimidated by those parties against goodness, you must never let it discourage you. That is because, by the Will of God, the people who strive for goodness will certainly triumph over those who are wicked. **So, you must unite with these "good" people, who are sincere, compassionate, true, just, honest, merciful, tolerant, fair, optimistic, charitable, unpretentious and forgiving, and offer them all your support.**

When you look around, as well as the good, you can also identify the evil ones and the type of society they intend to establish. In our day, the "evil ones" have established an apparently powerful alliance, and most likely, through their various methods, have silenced and intimidated many people advocating good morals. Behind all the evil you are not willing to acknowledge around, but which you can nonetheless not avoid, namely tyranny, corruption, disaffection, hatred, mercilessness, injustice, poverty, gossip, everything that upsets, annoys and distresses people, lies this concerted alliance of the evil.

The good and conscientious should never remain indifferent to this ever-present menace. If this evil moves you at all and you hope for a trouble-free world, then you are evidently a person of conscience. Thus, before vice takes hold of you and blunts your conscience, you should ally yourself with the good, and for the rest of your life, devote all your efforts to this cause. **Never forget that turning a blind eye to oppression and watching from the sidelines is oppression.**

No one should muffle his own voice with the excuse: "will my effort be of any help?", because it is one's inner intentions and sincere efforts which ultimately make the difference. One's efforts to join forces with the good and strive for what is right will be rendered by God a means to abolish all this wickedness and the alliance the evil endeavour to establish. In a verse of the Qur'an, God stresses the necessity for the existence of people who will prevent the harm of evil on earth:

Why were there not, among the generations before you, persons possessed of balanced good sense, prohibiting (men) from mischief in the earth - except a few among them whom We saved (from harm)? Those who did wrong gladly pursued the life of luxury that they were given and were evildoers. (Surah Hud: 116)

This book is a call to those who want goodness to prevail, bidding them to engage in good deeds and ally with the good. However, this call is not made to someone or some people somewhere out there; but directly concerns you. Even if you had until now allied with the evil, this book calls you to repent and to be on the side of the good and live by true moral values until death comes upon you.

WHO ARE THE REAL GOOD AND THE REAL EVIL?

In all corners of the world, there is evil, injustice, tyranny and wrongdoing. There are a number of reasons why people are witness to these negative realities which have become part of our daily lives. From the time a person acquires consciousness, he is exposed to an outpouring of news about such terrible happenings. Hardly a day goes by without encountering stories in the papers or on the TV, of swindlers, cruel serial killers, unprotected women, children and the elderly abandoned mercilessly to hunger and cold, all harrowing reminders that immorality, corruption, conflicts of interests and degeneracy are firmly rooted in society.

The majority of people who witness such events consider them as events which befall others, and thus, as things that have no relevance to them. For this reason, they never assume responsibility for the unrest, corruption and mercilessness that affects society. For instance, it may be that an innocent and defenceless person is exploited by a wealthier one, who insults and slanders him. In such an instance, everyone would recognise that the wealthy person is guilty of unjustly mistreating the innocent person. However, often, most people prefer to remain silent. They simply say "What difference would my words make?" or "This is none of my business", and turn a blind eye to this unfairness.

Undoubtedly, such situations arouse strong feelings and move a person whose heart is not so hardened. However merely getting angry, and disapproving, or feeling distressed, will in no way prove to be a hindrance to the recurrence of these harms. For this end, those who are conscientious and wish for the good of humanity should put forth a sincere effort and in every circumstance, lend their support to others who also strive for the good.

However, in order to do so, one needs to be able to distinguish between the good and the evil. Today "goodness and evil" have become relative concepts, varying according to the society, the type of social lifestyle and interests. For example in our day, caring for stray dogs and protecting their rights is regarded as an important mark of goodness. Similarly, making a few phone calls to collect aid for a disaster-stricken territory is sufficient to be regarded as a charitable person. A person busying himself in his spare times with renovation of a school building, or meeting a few school children's needs, deems himself worthy of life-long honour and earns the respect and appreciation of the rest of society. Surely these can be considered acts of goodwill, yet, it is obvious that such feeble attempts are an insignificant contribution to the total eradication of all the wickedness that exists. As a matter of fact, these people also know that their efforts do not require great sacrifices. Some of them may even be aware that with such charity work, they can ingratiate themselves to people surrounding them, wanting to be admired for their efforts. Ultimately, another motivation for their interest in such charity work may be to ease their conscience.

However, the purpose of the "good", who are the subject of this book, is loftier and more noble. The "alliance of the good", formed by people committed unconditionally to remain among the good and offer complete support to this end, acquires immense strength and brings forth unprecedented results in the shortest possible time. Grudge, hatred, mercilessness, insincerity, lying, injustice, penetrating into the societies of the world today, can only be removed by the "alliance of the good". Only people with high morals can stop the harm such corruption brings to the world.

None of these goals should seem remote, imaginary or unattainable to the reader. As you read, you will also acknowledge that joining with the "alliance of the good" is amenable to anyone. Be they a housewife, a high school student, a tradesman, or a professor, every conscientious person living by moral principles and committed to the dissemination of such values in society is capable of associating with the good. For this end, you must set aside your prejudices, presuppositions, and the ideas of right and wrong you have acquired earlier in life. The next step will be to look around you to identify the true good and the true evil. In the process, you will have to adopt a single criterion: the Qur'an, the only guide sent to mankind by God. That is because, only God knows who are the truly good or the truly evil, and it is in the Qur'an that He provides us a detailed account of the attributes of the good and the evil.

The Good and the Evil in the Qur'an

The only reason why a man conducts himself immorally is a lack of faith in God and the Day of Judgement and a lack of fear for God. Think for a moment about all the evil on earth: injustice, jealousy, murders, grudge, hatred, mercilessness, deceit, malice, oppression... In the Qur'an, God prohibits man from exhibiting these traits and informs that people committing them will be exposed to eternal punishment in the hereafter. For this reason, it is unlikely that a God-fearing person exhibits "devilish" characteristic. One of the verses of God forbids evil as follows:

We have sent down the Book to you making all things clear and as guidance and mercy and good news for the Muslims. God commands justice and doing good and giving to relatives. And He forbids indecency and doing wrong and tyranny. He warns you so that hopefully you will pay heed. (Surat an-Nahl: 89-90)

You may hear people saying that they avoid those forms of mischief commonly practised in society though they do not believe in God and the Day of Judgement. However, it is a definite and evident fact that a person, who has never been involved in any wicked deed in his lifetime, may possibly suddenly change this attitude once changing conditions seriously challenge his interests. When his career, for which he has worked day and night, or his wealth or life are at stake, for instance, he does not hesitate to cause harm to another person. We often encounter such people in our every day lives. In business life, in fear of being fired from his job for a mistake he has made, a person may well put the blame on someone else. Alternatively, a person who as a principle never accepts bribes or does anything unlawful, may find it reasonable to take a bribe for something urgent, for instance, when he has to pay his son's hospital bills.

If a non-God fearing person claims to be the most reliable and virtuous person in the world, it would definitely not prove to be convincing. Such a person may truly avoid committing theft or lying but he may lack good morals. You may not find an amicable, sincere and compassionate attitude in him, for instance. He may humiliate people in words or with his jokes, and the way he talks to people may have a disturbing tone. Similarly, a non-gambling person may indulge in a game when he is in an environment where gambling is popular. It would be unreasonable to consider a non-God-fearing man a truly righteous person, since he has an inherently weak-will that is prone to temptation because of a lack of fear of God.

There are also those who relentlessly commit acts of immorality, disturb, degrade or defraud people, use abusive language, do not value people, think only of themselves, act aggressively and maliciously, and yet help the poor now and then. In such cases, we certainly cannot consider these people to be "good". The essential attributes of a good person are righteousness, honesty, justice, and sincerity. However we should also keep in mind that a good person who is sincere can also make mistakes and have certain failings, but what makes him different is his endeavour to purify himself of these flaws, and to exhibit moral perfection as best as he can. A person with fear of God shows good character, not only at particular times, but under all circumstances. His moral perfection is not dependent on the changing attitudes of people or of events and conditions around him, but the consideration of the heavy judgement awaiting in the hereafter, and facing an outcome from which there is no return. With these factors in mind, he cannot dare to say a word or commit anything for which he would fail to give account in the hereafter. On the contrary, he pursues the bounties he hopes to attain in the hereafter. In the Qur'an, God calls man to ponder over the Day of Judgement:

> **On the Day that each self finds the good it did, and the evil it did, present there in front of it, it will wish there were an age between it and then. God advises you to beware of Him. God is Ever-Gentle with His servants. (Surah Ali 'Imran: 30)**

Consequently, fear of God in one's heart is a sign of being among the good. A non-God fearing person who does not observe God's limits inevitably identifies himself with the alliance of the evil. Possibly, he does not always actively participate in this wicked alliance, but, considering that conditions may develop at any time to in such a way as to prepare the appropriate ground for becoming involved in acts of wickednesss, he may, deliberately or not, side with the evil ones against the good.

God informs believers who the worst people are: **"The worst of creatures in the sight of God are those who disbelieve. They will not believe."** (Surat al-Anfal: 55). Therefore, someone who wants to ally with the good should definitely be with God-fearing people.

One's Behaviours Display His True Intention

In one's efforts to distinguish the good from the evil, an important point needs also to be considered: despite the fact that a great number of people say they believe in God and the Qur'an, in the way they live their lives and their attitudes, they are at variance with Qur'anic principles. In Surat al-Baqara, God reveals the real nature of those who claim to believe in God and the hereafter and yet do nothing but commit mischief:

Among the people there are some who say, 'We believe in God and the Last Day,' when they are not believers. They think they deceive God and those who believe. They deceive no one but themselves but they are not aware of it. There is a sickness in their hearts and God has increased their sickness. They will have a painful punishment on account of their denial. When they are told, 'Do not cause corruption on the earth,' they say, 'We are only putting things right.' No indeed! They are the corrupters, but they are not aware of it. When they are told, 'Believe in the way that the people believe' they say, 'What! Are we to believe in the way that fools believe?' No indeed! They are the fools, but they do not know it. When they meet those who believe, they say, 'We believe.' But then when they go apart with their satans, they say, 'We are really with you. We were only mocking.' But God is mocking them, and drawing them on, as they wander blindly in their excessive insolence. Those are the people who have sold guidance for misguidance. Their trade has brought no profit; they are not guided.
(Surat al-Baqara: 8-16)

As these verses also inform, such people maintain that they are rightful, honest and virtuous, and frequently condemn the immoral behaviour of others around them and warn them otherwise. However, they are actually the ones who spread mischief on earth, who do wrong secretly and deviously, who create conflict and stir up enmity among people. For this reason, in our criterion to establish the good and the evil, we should pay attention that people's acts match their words. The Prophet Muhammad's (peace be upon him) following words explain this very well:

Actions are only by intentions, and every man has only that which he intended. Whoever's emigration is for God and His Messenger then his emigration is for God and His Messenger. Whoever's emigration is for some worldly gain which he can acquire or a woman he will marry then his emigration is for that for which he emigrated.

For instance, one would naturally raise doubts about the sincerity of a person who claims to be a Muslim if he were to wage a covert struggle against Muslims. If a person, for instance, who claims that he attaches much importance to moral values, and looks for honesty and sincerity in people, advocates indecent people known for their immorality, and presents them as respectable people who have unimpeachable attributes, then this would cast doubts on such a person's sincerity. Rather, the actual purpose of those who associate the concept of immorality with "courage", "modernism", "elitism" and "freedom" is evident. They tempt people with such terms to make them see immorality as a virtue and to indulge in degeneracy.

In the Qur'an, God makes plain who the good and the evil are, as well as their attributes, lifestyles, mindset and outlook on life and other people. A person who is sincerely in pursuit of goodness should first identify the attributes of the good in the Qur'an, and accordingly, search for these features in those surrounding him. The same thing also applies in identifying the evil. Some of the attributes of the evil of which God makes clear in the Qur'an are as follows:

* Sinful
* Consumes ill-gotten gains
* Associates partners with God
* Disrespectful and disloyal to parents
* Readily kills an innocent person for personal gains
* Enjoins evil
* Hinders from good
* Greedy
* Rarely ever remembers God
* Despicable
* Slanderer
* Perpetrator of calumnies
* Forbidder of good
* Transgressing beyond bounds

* Violent-cruel when God's verses are recited, or interrupts discussions of religion saying "(These are) the myths of the ancient peoples"

* Murders people for a small piece of land or source of water, drives away children, the elderly, and women and men out of their land, subjects them to torture and keeps silent about those who commit all such cruelty

* Believes in some parts of the Qur'an and disbelieves the rest
* Commits mischief on earth
* Causes unrest in society
* Mocks people or societies
* Abuses peoples' reputations
* Gossips
* Slanders
* Snoops or spies on people

* Bases his judgements about people on conjecture and spreads such false information which sometimes leads to provocation

* Cruel, ignorant, selfish
* Offends people with harsh criticisms
* Treacherous
* Pretentious
* Heedless
* Liar
* Rebellious
* Unable to use common sense
* Does not listen to advice
* Pessimistic
* Despairing
* Stubborn
* Prideful
* Arrogant
* Resists what is right and correct
* Ungrateful
* Sceptic

Some of the traits of the good of which God informs in the Qur'an are the following:

* Believes in God, the Day of Judgement, angels, the Book and the prophets
* Repels evil with good
* Pays the poor-rate (zakat)
* Observes the limits set by God
* Spends wealth out of love for God, towards relatives, orphans, the needy, and for the wayfarer and those who ask
* Establishes regular prayers (salaat)
* Keeps promises and obligations
* Patient in distress and affliction and in times of conflict
* Loyal, honest, sincere, kind, compassionate, protective and righteous
* Concerned
* Respectful of believers
* Has sound reasoning
* Honourable
* Conscientious ÆTrustworthy
* Clean
* Obedient
* Humble
* True to his promise
* Kind-natured
* Turns to God with devotion
* Endowed with constancy
* Persevering
* Submits himself to God ÆPerceptive
* Speaks wisely
* Respected
* Self-respecting
* Not fearing the censure of any censurer
* Brave
* Keeps to a moderate course

* Tolerant
* Compassionate
* Honourable
* Gives glad tidings
* Happy and fortunate
* Courteous
* Speaks graciously to people
* Decent
* Virtuous
* Turns to God alone

When those people who lack these attributes of believers mentioned in the Qur'an , and on the contrary, adopt wicked manners in their conduct, claim that they behave in the name of "goodness", state that they are against wrongfulness while they do wrong against people, condemn slanderers while they themselves slander other people, or claim to be innocent and honest while they are definitely fraudulent, provide clear signs of their insincerity and hypocrisy.

Consequently, someone who is committed to ally himself with the good should make a careful examination of all that happens around him, and while arriving at a decision, base his conclusions on the criteria established by the Qur'an rather than what the majority think.

The Evil Ones Follow Satan's Way

The majority of people believe Satan to be an "imaginary" being with no real existence, and merely a concept symbolising evil. However, God also created the jinn, angels and Satan, as He created man and all the other living beings on earth, though in another dimension.

The most obvious characteristics of Satan are his disobedience to God and his arrogance. These aside, from the time God created the first human being, namely Prophet Adam (as), on earth, Satan set himself to lead people astray and hinder them from the right path. This is revealed in the Qur'an as follows:

He said, 'By Your might, I will mislead all of them except for Your chosen servants among them.' (Surah Sad: 82-83)

Satan has various methods he uses to prevent people from following their conscience and from the righteous way of God. He may instil in them apprehensions or direct people to what is wrong by way of his friends. Take, for instance, a person who recently started performing his regular prayers or complying with the commandments of God. Some of his friends, who are under the influence of Satan, may ridicule this person or draw his attention to some other temptation at prayer times. If this person fails to have a strong will and commitment to his conscience, then Satan may, within a short time, make this person stop practising his prayers by way of his friends. Alternately, a person helping the poor may be called a "fool" by his immediate circle and be convinced into spending his money instead on a new car or a holiday. Satan, using the people around him, may make this person see righteous deeds as somewhat difficult to follow or even wicked, and thus prevent him from engaging in acts of goodness. At times, Satan makes one abandon one's best friends in their most difficult times, so that his own interests are not effected. In such a case, a person faces a dilemma from which he has difficulty finding a way out. Attempting to be conscientious, he feels he has to help his friend through a difficult time. On the other hand, he cannot free himself from the grip of personal financial concerns or other difficulties he would face if he decided to offer his help. When considering a course of action, a person usually assumes he is merely in the process of making certain decisions and evaluating certain options. However, the dilemma he experiences does not result merely from conflicting ideas, but rather, it is a struggle between the voice of his conscience and that of Satan.

In brief, either by directly whispering to the mind or by way of certain people, Satan infuses man with negative inspirations, hinders him from conforming to God's way and following his own conscience, from engaging in good deeds, and talking graciously or making sacrifices. Those following in the footsteps of Satan, either deliberately or unintentionally, naturally take sides with him and throughout their lives remain among the evil. In the Qur'an, God explains the influence of Satan on man as follows:

You who believe! Do not follow in the footsteps of Satan. Anyone who follows in Satan's footsteps should know that he commands indecency and wrongdoing. Were it not for God's favour to you and His mercy, not one of you would ever have been purified. But God purifies whoever He wills. God is All-Hearing, All-Knowing. (Surat an-Nur: 21)

Satan has gained mastery over them and made them forget the remembrance of God. Such people are the party of Satan. No indeed! It is the party of Satan who are the losers.
(Surat al-Mujadila: 19)

Satan carries on a similar struggle against all people, but people who have fear of God, who guard against evil, conform to their conscience, and have a strong will, are not led astray by him. Weak-willed people having no deep-rooted fear for God, however, are tempted by Satan as the verses of God inform. In the following verse, the characteristics of the people who come under the influence of Satan are related:

Shall I tell you upon whom the Satans descend? They descend on every evil liar. They give them a hearing and most of them are liars. (Surat ash-Shu'ara': 221-223)

Those under the influence of Satan and who have gone astray usually present themselves as good and charitable people. However, their attitude towards people, and the lack of love, compassion and tolerance in their hearts, reveals that Satan has absolute control over them. This is related in a verse as follows:

If someone shuts his eyes to the remembrance of the All-Merciful, We assign him a Satan who becomes his bosom friend - they debar them from the path, yet they still think they are guided. (Surat az-Zukhruf: 36-37)

How do the Evil Ones Come Together?

For the evil ones to unite and carry out activities against believers, they first have to find each other. They do not require any effort for this purpose. The alliance emerges spontaneously, and in the normal course of daily life. The appropriate ground has already been laid by Satan through various methods and tactics.

Everything, from the people who would ally against the good to the timing or the type of plots hatched are all predetermined. Never is a call made for this unification. The call is already inspired by Satan in the hearts of those "who carry discord in their hearts". Thus, without effort, they come together, hatch plots and plan their evil actions. In daily life, they hear the call of disbelievers and identify themselves with the evil. The grudge they feel towards the believers and the vehement hatred overflowing their heart are the source of this unification. God gives an account of the grudge disbelievers nurse in their hearts against the believers and warns them thus:

You who believe! Do not take any outside yourselves as intimates. They will do anything to harm you. They love what causes you distress. Hatred has appeared out of their mouths, but what their breasts hide is far worse. We have made the Signs clear to you if you use your intellect. There you are, loving them when they do not love you, even though you believe in all the Books. When they meet you, they say, 'We believe.' But when they leave they bite their fingers out of rage against you. Say, 'Die in your rage.' God knows what your hearts contain. (Surah Ali 'Imran: 118-119)

While establishing their unification, they look for certain traits in a person; he has to turn away from God's religion, turn a blind eye to wickedness, readily commit evil acts, all the while, not feeling any pangs of conscience. The presence of a person who lives by the moral values of the Qur'an upsets the evil ones greatly. Hearing a single word reminding them of good character, righteousness, or honesty, is intolerable since such words would evoke the voice of their conscience which they never wish to hear. That is the reason why the wicked only enjoy the company of the wicked. They are made happy by the presence of the wicked. They greatly wish for the strengthening of their evil union since they know a strong alliance of the good would harm them. For instance, a thief enjoys the company of thieves. Alternatively, homosexuals all speak the same language. No matter where they are, they find each other and are rarely apart from one another. That is because they are never despised for their wickedness among their own, but rather, are encouraged by people sharing the same values. A person who slanders innocent people only feels at ease when he is surrounded with slanderers like himself. He listens to their views, boasts about his "accomplishments" and asks for their advice. In return, his companions tell him about their own immorality, the cruelty they have committed and the slandering they have done.

So, what is meant by the alliance of the evil is this attraction of the wicked to one another. If there is anyone around who questions their wicked deeds, it terribly annoys them. That is why they never want to see such person around, and why the evil ones only enjoy the company of one another.

The Evil Avoid Being With The Good and Feel Enmity Towards Them

We have stressed many times that the evil ones behave under the inspiration of Satan. Whether they admit this fact or not, you can recognize the influence of Satan in their words, attitudes and decisions. That is why their attitude towards the good is the same as Satan's. Even before the wicked were created, Satan had rejected the company of the good and waged an unrelenting struggle against them. God makes this posture of Satan clear in the following verses:

Then the angels prostrated all together, every one of them – except Iblis. He disdained to be one of the prostrators. He said, 'Iblis, what is it that prevents you being among the prostrators?

'He said, 'I will not prostrate to a human being whom You have created out of dried clay formed from fetid black mud.' (Surat al-Hijr: 30-33)

At a closer look, we also see that the essential characteristics of evil people today is also an insistence on avoiding the good, an obnoxious attitude towards them, arrogance, disobedience and rebellion. On top of all that, Satan is firmly committed to averting people from goodness and what is beautiful, and to leading them astray.

All of these indicate that those who strive together against goodness and try to eradicate the faith people have in God and the Hereafter, and moral values like sacrifice and loyalty, share the same common traits. However, it is impossible for these people to attain success; both in this world and beyond. God will pay them back what they deserve. That is because God is the friend and protector of His true servants:

God is the Protector of those who believe. He brings them out of the darkness into the light. But those who are disbelievers have false gods as protectors. They take them from the light into the darkness. Those are the Companions of the Fire remaining in it timelessly, for ever. (Surat al-Baqara: 257)

THE REAL GOAL OF
THE EVIL'S ALLIANCE

Out of inherent jealousy and rivalry, selfish, ambitious, unscrupulous and malicious people can never take a joint action or co-operate. As a result, factions emerge among them which cause still more enmity between one another. In a verse this trait of the disbelievers is stated as follows:

... Their hostility towards each other is intense. You consider them united but their hearts are scattered wide. That is because they are people who do not use their intellect.

(Surat al-Hashr: 14)

Nevertheless, despite the existence of these factions among them, some factors bring the evil together and make them act in unison. Before anything else, what makes them come together and unite for a common goal is, as mentioned in earlier sections, the influence of Satan has on the wicked ones. Their unification is not dependant on a call, a declaration or a written agreement. Indeed, in most cases, not a word is spoken or a meeting held to establish a strong unity. Even those among whom there is constant competition, or who have problems with each other due to conflict of interests, forget all about their differences when a common goal is in question, and decide to unite. This goal is the one commanded by Satan: to form a joint force against the good, against Muslims who believe in

God and the hereafter, sincere, conscientious and honest people who are on the side of justice. In this way, they want to coerce the good to their side…God gives an account of this secret call of Satan in the verse; "…The Satans inspire their friends to dispute with you…"(Surat al-An'am: 121)

The ultimate aim of this alliance, shaped by the efforts and inspiration of Satan, does not differ from the goals of the evil of the past.

Both in the past and today, the main goal of the alliance of the evil is to hinder the diffusion of moral values, like self-sacrifice, sincerity, honesty, conscientiousness and justice among people. No matter how such people strive to present themselves as the advocates of goodness, and living by the principles of the Qur'an, these values will always remain an impediment to their attainment of their personal ambitions, that is, they do not suit their purposes. This is the underlying reason why they exert such an all-out effort to obstruct the spread of the Qur'anic principles and desire to have fewer good people around. Meanwhile, they wish the good to become diverted from the right path, and to join them. They always wish them to disregard the truth and pursue trivial aims and desires, as do the wicked, and become people who live only to eat, drink and enjoy themselves. Once the good start talking, thinking and writing like them, and conduct themselves towards the young, children and elderly in a like manner, they will be satisfied and stop opposing them. In several verses, God informs us that disbelievers are deeply committed to the idea of making the good side with themselves:

They would like you to disbelieve just as they disbelieve so that you will all be the same…(Surat an-Nisa': 89)

If they come upon you, they will be your enemies and stretch out their hands and tongues against you with evil intent, and they would dearly love you to disbelieve.
(Surat al-Mumtahana: 2)

Many of the People of the Book would love it if they could make you revert to disbelief after you have believed, showing innate envy now that the truth is clear to them. But you should pardon and overlook until God gives His command. Truly God has power over all things. (Surat al-Baqara: 109)

God informs in another verse that disbelievers would continue striving until they divert the believers from their religion:

...but barring access to the Way of God and rejecting Him and barring access to the Masjid al-Haram and expelling its people from it are far more serious in the sight of God. Tumult is worse than killing. They will not stop fighting you until they make you revert from your religion, if they are able. As for any of you who revert from their religion and die while they are disbelievers, their actions will come to nothing in the world and the hereafter. They are the Companions of the Fire, remaining in it timelessly, for ever. (Surat al-Baqara: 217)

Another primary goal of the alliance of the evil is to hinder believers from performing good deeds through various methods, if they fail to draw them to their own side. Information about the former nations constitute important part of the Qur'an, informing us about their methods, which range from slander, to arrest, threat, murder, assassination, massacre, exile, mockery, humiliation, and wreaking the unity of the believers. Some such verses are as follows:

As for those who have set up a mosque, causing harm and out of disbelief, to create division between the believers, and in readiness for those who previously made war on God and His Messenger, they will swear, 'We only desired the best.' But God bears witness that they are truly liars. (Surat at-Tawba: 107)

Before them the people of Noah denied the truth. They denied Our servant, saying, 'He is madman, 'and he was driven away with jeers. (Surat al-Qamar: 9)

God merely forbids you from taking as friends those who have fought you in the religion and driven you from your homes and who supported your expulsion. Any who take them as friends are wrongdoers. (Surat al-Mumtahana: 9)

However, it should not be forgotten that in the Qur'an, God makes it clear that futile are the strivings of those who drift away from the religion of God and revolt against His messengers:

The people of Noah denied the truth before them, and the Confederates after them. Every nation planned to seize its Messenger and used false arguments to rebut the truth. So I seized them, and how was My retribution! (Surah Ghafir: 5)

LEADERS OF THE EVIL'S ALLIANCE

In the Qur'an, God states that the doers of mischief on earth, who are struggling to hinder believers from their noble cause, are guided by certain people who are, in Qur'anic terms, called the "the chiefs of the nation". A close read of the Qur'an reveals that such leaders existed in every society and throughout history. These people attempted to provoke the masses against believers and, deriving power from their prosperity and social status, remained arrogant, aggressive and unyielding. In the face of these leaders' apparent grandeur, based on wealth and temporal power, people generally feared them, and out of this fear, followed their way. As the Qur'an informs, however, complying with these people, and putting one's trust in them without listening to the voice of one's conscience, will be a reason to be dragged into hellfire. God explains this fact in His verses as follows:

> We sent Moses with Our Signs and clear authority to Pharaoh and his ruling circle. They followed Pharaoh's command but Pharaoh's command was not rightly guided. (Surah Hud: 96-97) We made them leaders, summoning to the Fire, and on the Day of Rising they will not be helped. We pursued them with a curse in this world and on the Day of Rising they will be hideous and spurned. (Surat al-Qasas: 41-42)

Those causing unrest and corruption in society are some of the people who hold power and wealth. This is expressed in a verse as follows:

When We desire to destroy a city, We send a command to the affluent in it and they become deviant in it and the Word is justly carried out against it and We annihilate it completely. (Surat al-Isra': 16)

And Thus have We placed leaders in every town, its wicked men, to plot in it. They plot against themselves alone, but they are not aware of it. (Surat al-An'am: 123)

When we talk about the leaders of a society, the first thing that occurs to our mind is the wealth they hold, and the power they wield through such wealth. These people, who maintain under their control some of the most important institutions that constitute the social structure of societies, can thus indoctrinate masses without difficulty and impose on them their life style and outlook which is far removed from Qur'anic values. Another method they use is to intimidate the good by way of their power. This trait in leaders is stated in the following verse:

No one had belief in Moses except for a few of his people out of fear that Pharaoh, and the elders, would persecute them. Pharaoh was high and mighty in the land. He was one of the profligate. (Surah Yunus: 83)

The masterminds of this evil alliance and those directing it are actually those leaders who have influence over the masses. Coming together, these leaders ally against the good; and scheme to defeat them or to render them ineffective. In their endeavour, they receive help from those people sharing the same views. A story about Moses in the Qur'an provides examples:

A man came running from the furthest part of the city, saying, 'Moses, the Council are conspiring to kill you, so leave! I am someone who brings you good advice.' (Surat al-Qasas: 20)

So Pharaoh went away and concocted his scheme and then he arrived. (Surah Ta ha: 60)

As these verses also state, the leaders of the evil ones gather and take decisions against the good, and enhance their alliance by bringing together those whom they hope to use against the good. Throughout history, those following the evil alliance, either out of fear, timidity or by being impressed by its power, followed the leaders of the evil. For instance, those who were ruthless enough to massacre millions of innocent people under the command of leaders like the Pharaoh, Mao, Hitler, Stalin and Pol Pot, or those who joined terrorist groups and killed people, would also maintain that they committed such acts because they feared the cruelty of their leaders or were impressed by their power. In this world, there may be some people who may be fooled by their insincere explanations. In the hereafter, however, these explanations will be rendered useless. Such is the ultimate end of the wicked and their leaders:

He (God) will say, 'Enter the Fire together with the nations of jinn and men who have passed away before you.' Each time a nation enters, it will curse its sister nation, until, when they are all gathered together in it, the last of them will say to the first, 'Our Lord, those are the ones who misguided us, so give them a double punishment in the Fire.' He will say, 'Each will receive double. But you do not know it.' The first of them will say to the last, 'You are in no way superior to us so taste the punishment for what you earned.' As for those who deny Our Signs and are arrogant regarding them, the Gates of Heaven will not be opened for them, and they will not enter the Garden until a camel goes through a needle's eye. That is how We repay the evildoers. (Surat al-A'raf: 38-40)

However, the power held by the leaders of the disbelievers would then bring neither benefit nor harm to them or the people following them. The possessor of all might and property is our Lord, God. No one can do any good or any harm to another person unless by the Will of God. Throughout history, believers having faith in this truth remained neither under the influence of Pharaoh, nor Nimrod, nor any other evil leader. Fearing God alone, they always sought God's good pleasure and firmly guarded against evil. For instance, in the Qur'an God informs us that the majority of the people of

Moses feared the cruelty of the Pharaoh and his immediate circle, and hence, did not submit to the right path. Only a few young people took sides with Moses. Similarly, the magicians assigned by Pharaoh to hatch a plot against the prophet Moses (as) saw the truth and immediately followed him. Pharaoh's threats did not alter the belief of these brave and faithful followers. The good conduct of the magicians is told in the Qur'an:

The magicians threw themselves down in prostration. They said, 'We believe in the Lord of all the worlds, the Lord of Moses and Aaron.' Pharaoh said, 'Have you believed in him before I authorised you to do so? This is just some plot you have concocted in the city to drive its people from it. I will cut off your alternate hands and feet and then I will crucify every one of you.' They said, 'We are returning to our Lord. You are only avenging yourself on us because we believed in our Lord's Signs when they came to us. Our Lord, pour down steadfastness upon us and take us back to You as Muslims.' (Surat al-A'raf: 120-126)

As these verses make clear, no condition, threat, or attack, can hinder the alliance of those who are sincere and conscientious. In the same way as the wicked have leaders luring them to wickedness, insolence, and ultimately to hell, so the good have people guiding them to the truth, to the good pleasure of God, and God's compassion and Paradise. Some verses make mention of those who summon people to goodness:

And in addition to that We gave him Isaac and Jacob and made both of them righteous men. We made them leaders, guiding by Our command, and revealed to them how to do good actions and establish prayer and pay alms, and they worshipped Us. (Surat al-Anbiya': 72-73)

We appointed leaders from among them, guiding by Our command when they were steadfast and when they had certainty about Our Signs. (Surat as-Sajda: 24)

These were the righteous people who throughout their lives summoned mankind to faith and the right path of God.

THE INTRICACIES OF THE EVIL'S ALLIANCE

As stressed throughout the book, that the evil ally themselves against the good to render them ineffective, and that they will strive to do harm to them, is a fact proclaimed in the Qur'an. God has made clear in several verses that people complying with the call of Satan will expend great effort to hinder people from living by the principles of the Qur'an. That is the reason why the good must always be alert and cautious of evil, and interpret all that happens around them in the light of the Qur'an.

However, we must not forget that everything occurs within the destiny ordained by God, and that nothing happens by coincidence. There is a good and a divine purpose in such an alliance formed against sincere and conscientious people. God will reveal the good and purpose in such evil plans when He wills; either in this world or the hereafter. Accordingly, believers must remember that **"... God will not give the disbeliever any way against the believer."**(Surat an-Nisa':14). It is confirmed in other verses that God will help His good servants:

> **Those who were expelled from their homes without any right, merely for saying, 'Our Lord is God'. If God had not driven some people back by means of others, monasteries, churches,**

synagogues and mosques, where God's name is mentioned much, would have been pulled down and destroyed. God will certainly help those who help Him -God is All-Strong, Almighty; Those who, if We establish them firmly on the earth, will establish salat (regular prayer) and pay zakat (regular charity), and command what is right and forbid what is wrong. The end result of all affairs is with God. (Surat al-Hajj: 40-41)

Though we must bear in mind that the activities carried out by the collaboration of the wicked are complex, the fact remains that a person who interprets the world according to the Qur'an will have no difficulty in recognising these intricacies, and grasp that many of the events he once took for granted are in reality part of a plan implemented by the wicked. In the following pages, a number of examples of the devious and subtle approaches of the alliance of the evil will be provided. The purpose here is to help the sincere servants of God to recognise the evil around them and to show them a way out.

The Evil Try to Harm the Good by Speaking Out Against Them

The most apparent trait of an insincere and devious person is his presenting of himself as a totally different person. He seems to oppose immorality, rebellion, disloyalty, prostitution, and similar forms of wickedness, while he himself lives a despicable life. Typically, such a person, would one day act as a fervent advocator of religious values, and another as a guardian of chastity, who sternly condemns others for their immoral conduct. As if he were the most honest or sincere person on earth, he would criticise the deceitful conduct of others, even as far as saying he is astounded by such immoral conduct and condemn it. Those who are unable to consider such things carefully and who readily accept anything they hear and see, are likely to be deceived by the type of person who feigns "innocence and goodness".

These "phony righteous" people see themselves as the ones who "put society aright". However, they are the real perverted ones who encourage people into immorality. God informs us about the state of these people as follows:

> When they are told, 'Do not cause corruption on the earth,' they say, 'We are only putting things right.' No indeed! They are the corrupters, but they are not aware of it. (Surat al-Baqara: 11-12) How will it be when a disaster strikes them because of what they have done, and then they come to you swearing by God: 'We desired nothing but good and reconciliation'? (Surat an-Nisa': 62)

Another tactic employed by the evil to present themselves as good, virtuous, honest and sympathetic, is to speak ill of the truly good. While they chastise them, they also claim especially that they merely want to protect the public from the "evil" of such people. The Pharaoh is the most glaring example, and one who went down in history for this very aspect. The Pharaoh was a cruel, aggressive, vulgar, merciless, arrogant person who subjected his people to unbearable punishment and denied the existence of God. He strove to provoke his people against Moses, by showing him to be evil, and portraying himself as a person of "good intentions". This deceptive ploy of Pharaoh is mentioned in the Qur'an as follows:

> Pharaoh said, 'Let me kill Moses and let him call upon his Lord! I am afraid that he may change your religion and bring about corruption in the land.' (Surah Ghafir: 26)
> They said, 'These two magicians desire by their magic to expel you from your land and abolish your most excellent way of life, so decide on your scheme and then arrive together in force. He who gains the upper hand today will definitely prosper.' (Surah Ta ha: 63-64)

As stated in the above verses, Pharaoh attempted to make the prophet Moses (as) appear guilty in the eyes of the public, while assuming the role of a saviour and a self sacrificing person who cares for his subjects. Most likely, those people who did not act wisely, and who were not guided by their conscience, were deceived by the lies of the Pharaoh and sided with him. However, the truth is evident today; both who were the evil and who were the good of that time are now known to us. What is more important is that, God knows and sees everything. In the Hereafter, God's justice will prevail and the true good and evil will be apparent. Pharaoh hatched a plot against Moses but faced great disappointment both in this world and beyond. By the same token, those striving to show the good ones as evil, the trustworthy ones as traitors, and the loyal ones as liars, today have already committed themselves to a similar end, unless they repent and cease their evil ways. As God's messenger (peace be upon him) also said *"Accursed is he who harms a believer, or acts deceitfully towards him."*

We must also bear in mind that, no matter how they much strive to the contrary, the wicked ones cannot lure God's devoted servants to their side, nor make them resemble themselves. That is because, good and righteous people are far from what the evil say:

Corrupt women are for corrupt men and corrupt men are for corrupt women, good women are for good men and good men are for good women. The latter are innocent of what they say. They will have forgiveness and generous provision. (Surat an-Nur: 26)

For this reason, the evil, although greater in number, are always much weaker than the good. Being well aware that by nature believers are good and tender-hearted people, they can resort only to"slander". To this end, they exploit every possible opportunity.

As the Qur'an informs, throughout history, good and sincere people were blamed of sorcery, lying, opportunism, perversion, and subjected to various other forms of slander. That is why, in no period of history, believers who became the object of such slanderous accusations, were neither surprised nor upset. On the contrary, experiencing these events which also befell the prophets and true believers add to their zeal.

In the case of the Prophet Joseph (as), for instance, both his brothers and the wife of the master who adopted him plotted against him. However, there is a time, in absolutely certainty, when this plotting and slandering against believers will be punished. The slander made against Joseph by his brothers was the following:

They said, 'If he steals now, his brother stole before.' But Joseph kept it to himself and still did not disclose it to them, saying, 'The plight that you are in is worse than that. God knows best the matter you describe.' (Surah Yusuf: 77)

Those who raised false charges of adultery against Mary, and the honourable wife of our Prophet, and the ones who blamed other prophets with perversion and sorcery, all shared the same attitude. They knew without a doubt that the blessed people, who exhibited moral perfection throughout their lives, were far too virtuous and noble to commit any of these supposed misdeeds. However, only to degrade these noble people in the eyes of the public, and to shatter the trust and commitment people placed in these true believers, they resorted to such lowly forms of slander. Some of the words disbelievers uttered according to this rationale are mentioned in the Qur'an as follows:

They are surprised that a warner should come to them from among themselves. The disbelievers say, 'This is a lying magician. Has he turned all the gods into One God? That is truly astonishing!' Their leaders went off saying, 'Carry on as you are! Hold fast to your gods. This is clearly something planned. We have not heard of this in the old religion. This is merely something contrived. Has the Reminder been sent down to him out of all of us?' They are in doubt about My Reminder. They have yet to taste My punishment. (Surah Sad: 4-8)

The ruling circle of his people said, 'We see you in flagrant error.' (Surat al-A'raf: 60)

However, these plots failed and ultimately back-fired. Believers, on the contrary, were publicly cleared of every accusation, and, as always, bore themselves with dignity. Prophet Joseph (as), who was charged with theft, for instance, was so evidently trustworthy that the King entrusted Egypt's entire stores to him. People spoke against Mary, accusing her of being unchaste, although she has been preferred over all women. Prophet Joseph (as) also became the subject of a similar slander, despite the fact that he was a noble person, who meticulously observed God's limits. God informs us in the Qur'an that in the afterlife the accusers will be punished for what they have done to the believers:

Those who have brought up such slander form a clique among you. Do not suppose it to be bad for you; rather it is good for you. Every one of them will incur the evil he has earned and whoever has assumed his leadership over them (through such gossiping) will have serious torment. (Surat an-Nur: 11)

And so that He might punish hypocritical men and women as well as associating men and women – those who think bad thoughts about God. They will suffer an evil turn of fate. God is angry with them, and has cursed them and prepared Hell for them. What an evil destination! (Surat al-Fath: 6)

The Wicked Employ All Their Resources Against the Good

Among the most recognised characteristics of disbelievers are greed and selfishness. Particularly, they avoid spending their money for a good cause. They are often reluctant to give away even a portion of their money and property to earn the good pleasure of God. However, when they are called to evil, they never avoid spending of what they have. Furthermore, each group within the alliance of evil competes with the others in inflicting the most harm on the good. They motivate those who may be slow or perhaps hesitant in hatching plots against the good, and make sure they spend as much energy as possible towards this cause.

These people, who never attempt to engage in anything good, strive to their utmost when it comes to something bad. God informs us in the following verse that they do not hesitate to spend their wealth for evil:

> **Those who are disbelieving spend their wealth barring access to the Way of God. They will spend it; then they will regret it; then they will be overthrown. Those who are disbelieving will be gathered into Hell. (Surat al-Anfal: 36)**

They Threaten the Good and Try To Intimidate Them

The evil alliance resort to threat and intimidation against the righteous, and thus, by frightening them, try to lead them astray of the right way. This method, frequently used against the good in the past, is being used likewise in our day. The most threatening alliance of evil known in history was established by Pharaoh and his immediate circle, of which we mentioned in previous sections. Pharaoh threatened the Prophet Moses (as) and his followers with torture and execution. Pharaoh's cruelty is referred to in the verses that follow:

> **Pharaoh said, 'Have you had belief in him before I authorised you to do so? This is just some plot you have concocted in the city to drive its people from it. I will cut off your alternate hands and feet and then I will crucify every one of you.' (Surat al-A'raf: 123-124)**

From the Qur'an we learn that, apart from death, believers were also threatened by the evil alliance with exile and loss of their property:

> **They were very near to scaring you from the land with the object of expelling you from it. But had they done so they would only have remained there a short time after you. (Surat al-Isra': 76)**

> **Do not lie in wait on every pathway, threatening people,**

barring those who believe from the Way of God, desiring to make it crooked. Remember when you were few and He increased your number: see the final fate of the corrupters! (Surat al-A'raf: 86)

The ruling circle of those of his people who were arrogant said, 'We will drive you out of our city, Shu'ayb, you and those who believe along with you, unless you return to our religion.' He (Shu'ayb) said, 'What, even though we detest it? (Surat al-A'raf: 88)

Disbelievers sometimes employ covert forms of threat. The tone of their speech sounds as if they are concerned with the good, safety and well-being of the good. They strongly advise the good not to collaborate with believers, and stress that that they say so to ensure their safety and well-being, and that otherwise, they will have to suffer the dire consequences. With this approach, they hope to imply that everyone who sides with the believers and supports them will get into trouble, undergo great tribulation, and suffer much loss. In addition, as a warning to others, they punish a few of the good through their various methods and broadcast their menacing message. On the other hand, they will never neglect to give promises to them to provide all forms of support and protection, on the condition of breaking with the good. The leaders of the Prophet Shu'ayb's (as) people also covertly threatened the followers of Shu'ayb:

The ruling circle of those of his people who were disbelieving said, 'If you follow Shu'ayb, you will definitely be lost.' (Surat al-A'raf: 90)

The true good, patient, brave and resistant believers, who were committed to their cause and harboured only the fear of God in their hearts, guarded against evil and ignored such threats. None of the threats or pressure employed by the disbelievers changed their attitude; they proceeded on the right way as commanded by God. The answer the Prophet Shu'ayb (as) gave to his people who had threatened him, and the words of magicians to the Pharaoh, are telling examples:

We would be inventing lies against God if we returned to your religion after God has saved us from it. We could never return to it unless God our Lord so willed. Our Lord encompasses everything in His knowledge. We have put our trust in God. Our Lord, judge between us and our people with truth. You are the best of judges.' (Surat al-A'raf: 89)

They said, 'We are returning to our Lord. You are only avenging yourself on us because we believed in our Lord's Signs when they came to us. Our Lord, pour down steadfastness upon us and take us back to You as Muslims.' (Surat al-A'raf: 125-126)

The Evil Try to Humiliate the Good Before the Eyes of People

Mocking believers and speaking ill of them are some of the methods adopted by the wicked against the righteous, in an attempt to humiliate believers and make them seem insignificant and worthless in the eyes of others. Their purpose in this case is to eradicate the good, to hinder the spread of moral values based on the teachings of the Qur'an, and prevent people from following their way.

The truly good, conscientious and sincere, also invite their fellow men to live by the same conscientiousness and sincerity. They are highly committed to communicating to them the blessings of Qur'anic morals, the reality of the Day of Judgement and the hereafter, and the importance of having fear for God. Their sincerity usually makes a positive impression on the majority of people, fostering faith in God, good morals, righteousness, blessings, conscientiousness, loyalty, support, respect and love. Those harbouring enmity towards one another or otherwise dissidenting people unite, thanks to the positive influence effected by the good.

No doubt, such improvements to society are not in accordance with the plan of the evil, the envious and those indulging in immorality. In order to reverse these positive effects, the evil mock the good, accuse them of insanity, shallow-mindedness, bigotry, deceit, imposture, the intention being to bring them into disrepute. They think the views and efforts of a person who is portrayed as insane or as a forger could no longer win people's respect. This is a tactic which has been employed for thousands of years by deceitful and devious people, all disbelievers and hypocrites, but which has never attained success.

History abounds with the stories of prophets, the followers of Prophet Muhammad (pbuh), Islamic scholars and true Muslims, who struggled for the good of humanity and the improvement of morality, and who constantly met insults and mockery. The insults and mockery only revealed the true hatred and jealousy the wicked felt for the good. God informs us that what they hide in their hearts is far worse than what they say:

You who believe! Do not take any outside yourselves as intimates. They will do anything to harm you. They love what causes you distress. Hatred has appeared out of their mouths, but what their breasts hide is far worse. We have made the Signs clear to you if you use your intellect. (Surah Ali 'Imran: 118)

As mentioned earlier, the underlying reason for the aggressive attitude and hatred felt by the wicked towards the good, is their not adhering to the wishes of the immoral and unscrupulous people who do not observe God's limits, and their considering God's commands and prohibitions over and above their own desires. Meeting a conscientious Muslim, who guards against evil and does not follow his ego (an-nafs), such people adopt an aggressive attitude and attempt to hurt him both physically and verbally.

One of the terms most frequently used by the evil in their attack on the good is that of "insanity". As is stated in the Qur'an, many true servants of God were accused of being insane. No doubt, the accusers were very well aware that these people were by no means lacking in reason. On the contrary, they knew very well that everyone of them was a highly intelligent person with high morals. Yet, as mentioned earlier, the intention of the accusers is to shatter the credibility of the good in the eyes of society. The Qur'an also informs us that throughout history, the prophets and the righteous have been accused of insanity:

> 'He is nothing but a man possessed so wait a while and see what happens to him.' He (Noah) said, 'My Lord, help me because of their calling me a liar!' (Surat al-Muminun: 25-26)
> The ruling circle of those of his people who were disbelieving said, 'We consider you a fool and think you are a liar.' He (Hud) said, 'My people, I am by no means a fool, but rather am a Messenger from the Lord of all the worlds, transmitting my Lord's Message to you, and I am a faithful counsellor to you.' (Surat al-A'raf: 66-68)

Other offensive methods disbelievers employ to humiliate the good is to insult them and call them and their associates foolish, weak and shallow-minded, so as to portray them as ordinary, simple and even unimportant. These words, repeated by the evil throughout history, are related in the verses of the Qur'an. Some of those are as follows:

> When they are told, 'Believe in the way that the people believe, 'they say, 'What! Are we to believe in the way that fools believe?' No indeed! They are the fools, but they do not know it. (Surat al-Baqara: 13)
> The ruling circle of those of his people who were disbelieving said, 'We do not see you as anything but a human being like ourselves. We do not see anyone following you but the lowest of us, unthinkingly. We do not see you as superior to us. On the contrary, we consider you to be liars.' (Surah Hud: 27)
> They said, 'Shu'ayb, We do not understand much of what you say and we see you are weak among us. Were it not for your clan, we would have stoned you. We do not hold you in high esteem!' (Surah Hud: 91)

Wicked people are innately prone to using derision and sarcasm against the good. In this regard, both the good and sincere themselves, and the values they advocate, become the target of their derision. From the Qur'an, we learn that derision was something all the messengers encountered. This is the reason why a believer subjected to mockery knows it is something to endure with patience, following the example of the messengers of God, and hopes that it increases his reward in the hereafter. He is sure of one thing; that the mockery will ultimately overcome the one who ridicules, and that he will some day greatly regret what he had done.

Messengers before you were also mocked, but those who jeered were engulfed by what they mocked. (Surat al-Anbiya': 41)

They Strive to Spread Immorality and Diminish the Number of the Good

One of the hopes of the leaders of evil is to lead a carefree and indulgent life, for which they will not have to give account, and so not have to observe any limits. As we have discussed earlier, in doing so, they do not confess their real intentions, but instead employ deceitful methods to cover their aims.

Firstly, they associate themselves with a group that consists of people who respect no principles, who do not feel any shame, who openly perpetrate immoral acts and use vulgar language. These are the types of people who indulge in all forms of depravity, like homosexuality, prostitution, drugs or gambling. Nevertheless, regardless of their characteristics, some of them have earned positions of respect in society. They are often famous, or known as intellectuals or recognised for other talents. This being the case, their indulgence in immorality is regarded by the rest of society as acceptable. While otherwise socially inadmissible, contemptible and despicable manners and behaviour somehow become tolerated in society when they are associated with such people. The immoral behaviour exemplified by them becomes a defining feature of what is considered "bravery, modernity, freedom and intellectualism." This not being sufficient, these people are also presented as role models, especially to the young, as if they are living a good life. Ultimately, society abounds with those who imitate these people. Their clothing styles, make-up, their manner of speaking, the way they deal with people, and even their preferences in home decoration or social relations, are adopted by their followers. In this way, within a very short period of time the majority of the society is lured into this form of degeneracy.

This process develops so rapidly that manners and conduct one would not dare to consider or even to utter, in just a few years suddenly become socially acceptable. For instance, attitudes towards homosexuality, once a highly scorned and denounced practice, have changed dramatically in some social circles. It is no longer regarded as unusual to make close friends with homosexuals. Surely there exists an alliance somewhere that promotes this gradual transformation of social norms, by way of taking people within its sphere influence, through its concealed methods and organisations. It is the alliance of the evil.

Each and every member of this alliance, intentionally or otherwise, contributes to this degenerate propaganda, and supports its spread until the ultimate goal is finally attained. Considering the modern society of today, it would not be an exaggeration to say that certain fashion designers, film producers, song-writers, journalists, authors, movie directors, night club owners, etc. are involved in this alliance. (No need to say that there are always exceptions, with those who do not serve the purposes of this insidious alliance, and who remain conscientious and ally themselves with the good.)

Committed to spread wickedness in all domains of life, and to attract greater numbers of adherents to their alliance, the evil ones endeavour to keep the number of the good to the bare minimum. Yet, the fact remains that such efforts merely elevate the status of the good and increase the torment of the evil. God reveals this fact in His verses:

People who love to see filth being spread about concerning those who believe will have a painful punishment both in the

People who love to see filth being spread about concerning those who believe will have a painful punishment both in the world and the hereafter. God knows and you do not know. (Surat an-Nur: 19)
They would not restrain one another from any of the wrong things that they did. How evil were the things they used to do! You see many of them taking those who disbelieve as their friends. What their lower selves have advanced for them is evil indeed, bringing God's anger down upon them. They will suffer punishment timelessly, for ever. (Surat al-Ma'ida: 79-80)

They Try to Make People Believe They are Right

As stressed throughout this book, today, the evil represent the majority in society, as it had also been in the past. Their narrow outlook makes them see this as a factor that makes them superior over the good. Being the majority misleads them into thinking they are more powerful. They assume that the attracting of many adherents proves their correctness. A person that had been misled in this manner was the Pharaoh. This false assumption of his is related in the following verses:

Pharaoh sent marshals into the cities: 'These people are a small group and we find them irritating and we constitute a vigilant majority.' We expelled them from gardens and springs, from treasures and a splendid situation. (Surat ash-Shu'ara': 53-58)

However the vanquishers were not the armies and the Pharaoh but the Prophet Moses (as) and his followers, who were driven out of their land, and who were oppressed and despised because they were in the minority.

Essentially, that those under the command of Pharaoh represented the majority by no means proved their rightness. From the Qur'an we learn that the majority put their faith not in what is right, but in what misleads one from the right path. Also, we learn that they are liars:

If you obeyed most of those on earth, they would misguide you from God's Way. They follow nothing but conjecture. They do nothing but lie. (Surat al-An'am: 116)

Moreover, the good, even if they are the minority, will always prevail over the evil ones, though they outnumber the good. God gives glad tidings of this in this verse:

'How many a small force has triumphed over a much greater one by God's permission! God is with the steadfast. (Surat al-Baqara: 249)

Ultimately, it is a fallacy and misconception when some put forward various excuses to the good saying, "but these are the beliefs, moral values and the life-style maintained by the majority". Therefore, we must keep in mind that adhering to the path the majority follow is not necessarily the safest way, since, as also stressed in the verses above, it is nothing but a grand delusion.

The Evil Make Provocations Against the Good

Another feature of the alliance of the evil is their provocations against the good. The evil provoke others against the good through their works, by inventing stories, spreading rumours, through slander, false and ridiculous analogies or gossip. In the Qur'an, it is stated that it was the leaders of the people of Pharaoh who assumed a provocative approach:

The ruling circle of Pharaoh's people said, 'Are you going to leave Moses and his people to cause corruption in the earth (Egypt) and abandon you and your gods?' He (Pharaoh) said, 'We will kill their sons and let their women live. We have absolute power over them!'

Moses said to his people, 'Seek help in God and be steadfast. The earth belongs to God. He bequeaths it to any of His servants He wills. The successful outcome is for those who have fear of God.' (Surat al-A'raf: 127-128)

As these verses suggest, at the time when Pharaoh almost allowed Moses and his adherents to leave, the leaders tried to change his mind by making up lies and unfounded slanders about Moses to provoke the Pharaoh into oppressing the prophet and his followers. As is evident in this example, the alliance of the evil always focuses its efforts on inciting the evil against the good.

God, in the Qur'an, relates the following about such people who spread rumours about the good:

If the hypocrites and those with sickness in their hearts and the rumour-mongers in Madina do not desist, We will set you onto them. Then they can only be your neighbours there a very short time. (Surat al-Ahzab: 60)

Another method the evil have employed for thousands of years to such an end has been to coax the good into a conflict against their brothers and friends. All civil wars, conflicts and senseless enmities that have come about in history, originated from the all-out efforts of the evil. As a result of the enmity stirred up by the provocation of the evil, fellow citizens, even close friends and brothers, struggled against each other, and tortured and killed one another.

Also, in our day, through publications, speeches, lobbying and diplomacy, such people stealthily manage to bring two countries into a war, or stir up enmity among a people by dividing a nation into factions. This is an evil scheme that turns brother against brother. The purpose is to weaken these countries by civil wars and internal conflict so as to reconcile the structure of the target countries to their own goals and ideologies.

Another method employed by the evil alliance against the good is, as mentioned in previous sections, to portray some of the good as wicked in the eyes of other good people. To this end, they initiate underhanded strategies, ranging from spreading unfounded accusations to outright insults, so as to make the disparaging message "Look! We have unmasked the good; as you see, they are not on the right way." The intention in this case is to prevent the good to come together, and to support and protect the oppressed.

However, people of conscience who are able to analyse these tactics, so as to recognise and avert the secret plans of the evil, thanks to their conscience and sound mind, will never be deceived by such tricks. God warns believers against the traits of the evil in many of His verses, for example:

You who believe! If a deviator brings you a report, scrutinize it carefully in case you attack people in ignorance and so come to greatly regret what you have done. (Surat al-Hujurat: 6)

God's Messenger, the Prophet Muhammad (pbuh), also said that *"To harbour good thoughts (about a brother) is a part of well-conducted worship."*, reminding Muslims to be on guard against the whisperings of Satan which tries to make mischief among the believers. Consequently, you should keep in mind that, even if the alliance of the evil has provoked a whole city, or even the whole world against the good, God protects and guards the good. No plot of the evil can hurt the good, scare or worry them, unless by the Will of God.

Alliance of the Evil is Based on Interests

The leaders of the evil make promises to people and offer them certain privileges in order to attract them to their side. In the Qur'an, a promise given by Pharaoh to the magicians is related as follows:

When the magicians came, they said to Pharaoh, 'Will we be rewarded if we are the winners?' He said, 'Yes, and in that case you will be among those brought near.' (Surat ash-Shu'ara': 41-42)

However we should also mention that the evil alliance is in reality based on a rather feeble foundation. Every member has certain stipulations or a price in mind in joining the alliance. If they feel their personal interests are at stake, they lose no time in breaking with the alliance. That is because this alliance is not established on just grounds, but on falsehood. Every individual who does not believe in God and the hereafter, who has no fear for God and does not guard against evil, is afflicted with certain weaknesses, which the leaders of the evil take advantage of in every way they can, and which they use to gain further supporters.

Also, in our day, promises of money, property, fame or status, are sufficient to convince most people to take action against the good. Accordingly, unless he has fear for God, a person who is offered such promises will readily become so cruel as to make up slanderous accusations or tell lies about an innocent and pure person whom he has never met.

Contrarily, those individuals who side with the good only seek the mercy, consent and paradise of God. This alliance is formed according to the one and only just path of God, and those who are truly good never demand a "price". No worldly gain can divert them from doing what is right. In this regard, believers are following the messengers' examples. In the Qur'an, the messengers addressed their people as follows:

My people! I do not ask you for any wage for it. My wage is the responsibility of Him who brought me into being. So will you not use your intellect? (Surah Hud: 51)

The Two-faced Members of the Evil Alliance: Hypocrites

The most errant and troublesome members of the evil alliance are the hypocrites. Hypocrites are those insincere people who dubiously present themselves as the allies of the good. From the Qur'an, we know that these people conduct themselves as believers outwardly, though they actually keep company with the evil. These people feign forthrightness and honesty while they are among the good, but in privacy, or once they return to their real allies, they disclose their true wicked intentions. God reveals this trait of the hypocrites in the Qur'an as follows:

They have the word, 'Obedience!' on their tongues but when they leave your presence, a group of them spend the night plotting to do other than what you say. God is recording their nocturnal plotting. So let them be and put your trust in God. God suffices as a Guardian. (Surat an-Nisa': 81)

When they meet those who believe, they say, 'We believe.' But then when they go apart with their satans, they say, 'We are really with you. We were only mocking.' But God is mocking them, and drawing them on, as they wander blindly in their excessive insolence. (Surat al-Baqara: 14-15)

There are two main reasons why hypocrites associate themselves with the good despite the fact that they are inwardly wicked. First, they want to spy on the good for the evil. Secondly, they endeavour to stir unrest and carry out mischief among the good, and provoke the wicked against the good. These devious aims of the hypocrites are related in several of the verses:

If they had gone out among you, they would have added nothing to you but confusion. They would have scurried about amongst you seeking to cause conflict between you, and among you there are some who would have listened to them. God knows the wrongdoers. (Surat at-Tawba: 47)

O Messenger! Do not be grieved by those who rush headlong into disbelief among those who say 'We believe' with their tongues when their hearts contain no belief. And among the Jews are those who listen to lies, listening to other people who have not come to you, distorting words from their proper meanings, saying, 'If you are given this, then take it. If you are not given it, then beware!' If God desires misguidance for someone, you cannot help him against God in any way. Those are the people whose hearts God does not want to purify. They will have disgrace in the world and in the hereafter they will have a terrible punishment. (Surah al-Ma'ida: 41)

The character of the hypocrites and their end is also referred to in the sayings of the Prophet Muhammad (pbuh):

On the Day of Resurrection, the one in the vilest of conditions will be a two-faced person. He says one thing (in favour) of one person and then another thing (in regard to the same affair) to another person.

We should still remember that, although these people seem to attain their goal in the short term, God definitely renders their striving futile and inflicts indefinable suffering on them both in this world and beyond.

In Secret Meetings They Take Action Against the Good

The alliance of evil generally prefers night as the opportune time to plot against the good. This is stated in many verses in the Qur'an. That night is the time for the wicked to congregate and implement their evil plans is stated in the verses as follows:

They try to conceal themselves from people, but they cannot conceal themselves from God. He is with them when they spend the night saying things which are not pleasing to Him. God encompasses everything they do. (Surat an-Nisa': 108)

Arrogant towards it (the Qur'an), talking arrant nonsense all night long. (Surat al-Muminun: 67)

In Surat an-Naml, God informs us about an event in the past, where a gang of nine men who committed mischief in a city where believers lived, and who at night would scheme in secret to attack them. The relevant verses are the following:

There was a group of nine men in the city causing corruption in the land and not putting things right. They said, 'Let us make an oath to one another by God that we will fall on him and his family in the night and then say to his protector, "We did not witness the destruction of his family and we are telling the truth."' (Surat an-Naml: 48-49)

As the verses reveal, these people devised secretive and malicious plans against believers but in return were confronted by the plot God prescribed for them. The end of those who harm the innocent and plot against them at night is stated in the following section of the same verses:

They hatched a plot and We hatched a plot while they were not aware. So look at the end result of all their plotting; We utterly destroyed them and their whole people! These are the ruins of their houses because of the wrong they did. There is certainly a Sign in that for people with knowledge. (Surat an-Naml: 50-52)

Another trait of the oppressors who focus all their efforts to harm the good and cause trouble for them, is their devising of plans secretly God states this in many verses:

Moses said to them, 'Woe to you! Do not fabricate lies against God or He will annihilate you with His punishment. Fabricators of lies are bound to fail.' They argued among themselves about the matter and had a secret conference. (Surah Ta Ha: 61-62)

There is no good in much of their secret talk, except in the case of those who enjoin charity, or what is right, or putting things right between people. If anyone does that, seeking the pleasure of God, We will give him an immense reward. (Surat an-Nisa': 114)

We know how they listen when they listen to you, and when they confer together secretly, and when the wrongdoers say, 'You are only following a man who is bewitched!' (Surat al-Isra': 47)

These people with no faith in God, nor the mental faculties to grasp His power, talk freely among themselves, assuming that nobody hears them while they talk nonsense in the dark, or while they conceive plots against the good. However, they are wrong. Actually, they can hide their secret and evil plans or talks from people, but God knows, sees and hears every sentence, every word, every detail of their plotting, even the very inner thoughts a person keeps to himself. They believe their devious plans will never come to light and that their victims will never be able to save themselves. Nevertheless, God thwarts their plans even before they are hatched, and hears every word they speak. No matter where they hide or how elaborate are the precautions they take, they can never evade God. Every word one says and every inner thought one may have is kept in the sight of God, and will be presented to him on the Day of Judgement. As such, those plotting against the good will also have to give account of their secretive plans. Therefore, those who hatch insidious plots at night in their secret meetings should keep in mind that God hears and sees everything. In one verse, God says:

Do you not see that God knows what is in the heavens and on the earth? Three men cannot confer together secretly without Him being the fourth of them, or five without Him being the sixth of them, or fewer than that or more without Him being with them wherever they are. Then He will inform them on the Day of Rising of what they did. God has knowledge of all things. (Surat al-Mujadila: 7)

The Alliance of the Evil Today HasIntensified Its Efforts

Throughout this book, we mentioned that the evil unite to eradicate religion and believers, and resort to numerous forms of oppression and pressure tactics to this end. The existence of people of faith is the main reason why the evil unite, because a believer is the representative of Islam, God's true religion, and the guarantee of implementation of the moral values of the Qur'an on earth. For the evil, the threat of such a possibility requires the immediate removal of believers. What hinders the evil ones from living by their system of unbelief and of evil morals are the limits set by God and the moral principles prescribed by His religion. It is to remove these hindrances that the disbelievers are so strongly committed to co-operating with one another. Wherever there is prostitution, bribery, imposture, gambling, swindling, cruelty to orphans and the poor, extravagance, lack of love and respect, immorality, there is the evil alliance.

We are living in a period when the alliance of the evil has intensified their efforts, and believers, along with the innocent, poor and weak people, in all corners of the world, have been subjected to more oppression and suffering than ever before. It is essential that believers assess this reality according to the guidance of the Qur'an. According to the Qur'an, turning a blind eye to the ongoing cruelty, not engaging in an ideological struggle against the evil, watching everything silently and remaining inconsiderate towards the ongoing suffering in the world, is great oppression in itself. Keeping silent about the repression and cruelty inflicted on the Muslims and people striving to spread the morals of the Qur'an, makes one a silent member of the cruel alliance, or worse still, a participator in it.

Glancing through newspapers or magazines should suffice to see the rapaciousness of this alliance. For instance, 10-15 years ago, homosexuality was accepted as completely unacceptable and was severely condemned. However, this fact has dramatically changed today, giving way to an actual advocacy of the rights of homosexuals, as far as presenting this perversion as modern and a normal and "personal preference". This outlook is propagated by the popular media and the entertainment world. The public's inculcation into similar immoral trends as perfectly acceptable "preferences", thus laying the groundwork for their further diffusion throughout society, is merely a consequence of the evil plans orchestrated by the alliance of the evil.

In this time, when gambling, prostitution, and murder evoke little reaction, it is essential that people wake-up to reality. This is a time when the good, who are already deprived of their essential rights and freedoms, are oppressed and unjustly treated, whereas swindlers, murderers and tyrants have the freedom to do what they want. If innocent and defenceless people are murdered all around the world, merely because they have faith in God and because they say they are Muslims, and again, if those who call themselves "Muslim" can remain ambivalent to all this suffering, and dares to refer to it with a smile on his face, then this is the work of the alliance of the evil. Restoring peace and securing welfare, happiness, justice, tolerance, love and respect in the world is only possible through recognition and adherence to the values of the Qur'an. It is the believers who are the living examples of this good character, and it will be the alliance of the good that will ensure the prevalance of the values of the Qur'an; this is the definite promise of God.

God has promised those of you who believe and do right actions that He will make them successors in the land as He

made those before them successors, and will firmly establish for them their religion with which He is pleased and give them, in place of their fear, security. 'They worship Me, not associating anything with Me.' Any who are disbelieving after that, such people are deviators. (Surat an-Nur: 55)

THE EVIL'S GREATEST FEAR
THE ALLIANCE OF
THE GOOD

The previous sections of this book stressed the fact that since time immemorial, the evil have been the perpetrators of mischief on earth, have oppressed people, and brought about unrest, insecurity, conflicts and enmity. It is also stressed that the evil have established a strong union to root evil in society. However, it would be a rather pessimistic and negative approach to assume that there is nothing that can be done to change this dismal reality.

A person who adheres to the Qur'an and lives by it does not succumb to such hopelessness, and under no circumstance does he turn a blind eye to the wrongs around him. A conscientious and thoughtful Muslim strives to save not only those around him, but the society he lives in, and even the rest of humanity, from violence, conflict, war, immorality and mischief in general. It is clear that sincerity, conscience, honesty, compassion, love and respect, will eradicate immorality and all wickedness. In other words, the unity and co-operation of the good will defeat the alliance of the evil. In a verse of the Qur'an, God gives glad tidings regarding this fact:

Rather We hurl the truth against falsehood and it cuts right through it and it vanishes clean away! Woe without end for you for what you portray! (Surat al-Anbiya': 18)

Therefore, aside from exposing the true threat the alliance of evil poses to humanity, most beneficial would be the conscientious and sincere coming together against the evil, to support one another and protect the poor and those who are oppressed. This is the approach adopted by those striving to attain the good pleasure of God, and is highly praised in the Qur'an;

...Those who believe in him and honour him and help him, and follow the light that has been sent down with him, they are the ones who are successful.' (Surat al-A'raf: 157)

In the above verse, God commands believers to support, help and defend His messengers. In a similar manner, believers should also support and defend one another.

The Believers are the Guardians of One Another

There are several verses in the Qur'an that relate to us of believers as the guardians of one another. The following is one of them:

And (as for) the believing men and the believing women, they are guardians of each other. They command what is right and forbid what is wrong, and establish prayer and pay alms, and obey God and His Messenger. They are the people on whom God will have mercy. God is Almighty, All-Wise. (Surat at-Tawba: 71)

The word "guardian" means intimate, protector, helper and supporter. In this sense, believers, honest, sincere and conscientious people with high moral values, should support each other, and be helpers and protectors of one another. Our Beloved Prophet (pbuh) also stated this in his following saying:

A believer is a mirror to another believer. A believer is a brother to another believer. He saves him from losses. He safeguards his interests in his absence.

The stories related in the Qur'an about the prophets provide many examples about this practice. Moses, for instance, killed a man by mistake when he sided with a man who was in trouble. Then, he had to run away from the city to save himself from the cruelty of the Pharaoh and the leaders of the city. This is related in the verses as follows:

A man came running from the furthest part of the city, saying, 'Moses, the Council are conspiring to kill you, so leave! I am someone who brings you good advice.' So he left there fearful and on his guard, saying, 'My Lord, rescue me from the people of the wrongdoers!' (Surat al-Qasas: 20-21)

The Prophet Moses (as) managed to leave the city through a man who helped him as a favour to him. He then reached a watering place in the land of Madyan and helped two women who kept back their flocks because they did not want to mix with the shepherds near the water. Upon their return home, the women mentioned to their father, the Prophet Shu'ayb (as), the help Moses had offered them. Upon this, Prophet Shu'ayb (as) invited prophet Moses to his home. This is revealed in the verses as follows:

One of them came walking shyly up to him and said, 'My father invites you so that he can pay you your wage for drawing water for us.' When he came to him and told him the whole story he said, 'Have no fear, you have escaped from wrongdoing people.' (Surat al-Qasas: 25)

Because Prophet Shu'ayb (as) recognized the inherent goodness and trustworthiness of the Prophet Moses (as), he helped him in his difficult time and allowed him to stay in his household and to work for him. Shu'ayb's manner sets an example for the good in protecting and guarding other good people who encounter hardship. Unless the good offer help and support to one another in times of adversity, then they will leave each another alone and unable to defend themselves against the cruel people. In a verse of the Qur'an, God commanded our Prophet (pbuh): **"...take the believers who follow you under your wing"** (Surat ash-Shu'ara': 215). Taking believers under one's wing, protecting them against dangers and difficulties is a command of our Lord, and also a Sunnah of our Prophet to follow.

The Good Should Avoid Bickering and Unite

Unity, cooperation, solidarity, friendship, self-sacrifice, support, and similar other qualities are some of the beautiful attributes which are the underlying foundation of the Qur'anic morality. This is stated in many sayings of Our Prophet (pbuh). One of them reads: *'Believers are like the different parts of a building, each one supporting the other.' Then he demonstrated what he meant by interlocking his fingers.*

The religion of Islam ensures the establishment of a better world where there is love, peace, tolerance and understanding to one another. Societies possessing these features experience rapid development and achieve greater power. Once unity and cooperation are attained, individuals of such a society could channel their strength and energy towards goodness and good deeds rather than into disputes, fights, conflicts and wars. Essentially, a cause to which people commit themselves and devote all their effort, power, zeal and support, both material and spiritual, results in an ultimate success and beauty. What is more important is that God gives glad tidings that individuals working in unity and solidarity for good will receive God's help, support and power. For this reason, God reminds believers not to dispute among themselves so as not to lose strength. The verse below makes this point clear:

Obey God and His Messenger and do not quarrel among yourselves lest you lose heart and your momentum disappear. And be steadfast. God is with the steadfast. (Surat al-Anfal: 46) Establishing unity among the righteous is an exalted virtue recommended by God. Especially in a time where evil has permeated every aspect of society, not a single evil feature like peevishness, resentment or bickering should be tolerated among the good. Putting forth effort to remove such evil influences and adopting a compromising and conciliatory attitude is a great act of worship

The believers are brothers, so make peace between your brothers and have fear of God so that hopefully you will gain mercy. (Surat al-Hujurat: 10)

Disputes, enmity, hatred and anger are the features of immoral conduct inspired by the evil. True Muslims never conduct themselves under the influence of these undesirable feelings; they have fear for God and are always modest, friendly, thoughtful and full of love in their relations. People who are not sincere in their cause may feel jealous of their closest friends and even of their own brothers and sisters. Each other's success may stir up feelings of envy in their hearts. On the contrary, a true Muslim takes pride in other believers' success, and is happy for them as if it were his own accomplishment, and feels grateful to God for the blessings He has granted believers. Furthermore, he supports them in their endeavour and offers guidance if necessary. Those lacking such morals, on the other hand, hamper the progress of others. Feelings of rivalry and jealousy spoil the good deeds engaged in to attain the good pleasure of God, and accordingly, ruins any beauty or blessings. God's Messenger, the Prophet Muhammad (pbuh), also drew attention to this point and advised the believers to guard against such bad manners:

Do not envy each other, do not bid against each other, do not hate each other, do not turn your backs on each other, and let none of you sell upon the sale of another. Be slaves of God, brothers. A Muslim is the brother of a Muslim, he does not wrong him, fail to assist him, lie to him nor despise him.

Said Nursi, also known as Bediuzzaman (the Wonder of the Age) who is one of the greatest Islamic scholars of the 20th century gives extensive reference to these issues in his Risale-i Nur collection, a commentary on the Qur'an. In the sincere style that is peculiar to him, Bediuzzaman relates that believers should strictly avoid corrupt feelings such as competitiveness when they strive for a common goal:

The service of the truth is like carrying and preserving a great and weighty treasure. Those who carry that trust on their shoulders will be happy and grateful whenever powerful hands rush to their aid. Far from being jealous, one should proudly applaud the superior strength, effectiveness and capacity of those who in upright love come forward to offer their help. Why then look on true brothers and self-sacrificing helpers in a spirit of rivalry, thus losing sincerity? You will be exposed to fearsome accusations in the eyes of the people of misguidance, such as pursuing worldly interest through religion, even though it is something a hundred times lower than you and your belief, earning your livelihood through the knowledge of truth and rivalling others in greed and acquisitiveness. The sole remedy for this disease is to accuse your own soul before others raise these charges, and always to take the side of your fellow, not your own soul.

As Bediuzzaman Said Nursi also states, offering one's service towards establishment of the moral values of the Qur'an can be seen as preserving a treasure for the believers; one that is extremely precious. To this invaluable service, everybody must provide his wholehearted support and help. Feeling jealous of another believer who offers his devoted and unwavering support, or considering him as a rival, is unacceptable for a true Muslim. A believer should be proud of others' commitment and provide his support.

Jealousy is an attribute of the evil alliance. The existence of such an evil trait among individuals collaborating for a righteous end does nothing but diminish the strength of the alliance. It is surely the evil alliance that benefits from such detriment. As Bediuzzaman says, the only cure for this illness is not following one's ego and always taking the side of one's fellow.

In the Risale-i Nur collection, Bediuzzaman draws a comparison between the machinery of a factory and believers. The harmonious and smooth functioning of this machinery is essential for a productive output. A similar harmony is also required in the co-operation among believers. Said Nursi explains that believers should avoid talk which could cause jealousy and bitterness as follows:

This is not to criticize your brothers who are employed in this service of the Qur'an, and not to excite their envy by displaying superior virtues. For just as one of man's hands cannot compete with the other, neither his heart see his spirit's faults. Each of his members completes the deficiencies of the others, veils their faults, assists their needs, and helps them out in their duties. Otherwise man's life would be extinguished, his spirit flee, and his body be dispersed. Similarly, the components of machinery in a factory cannot compete with one another in rivalry, take precedence over each other, or dominate each other. They cannot spy out one another's faults and criticize each other, destroy the other's eagerness for work, and cause them to become idle. They rather assist each other's motions with all their capacity in order to achieve the common goal; they march towards the aim of their creation in true solidarity and unity. Should even the slightest aggression or desire to dominate interfere, it would throw the factory into confusion, causing it to be without product or result. Then the factory's owner would demolish the factory entirely. And so, O Risale-i Nur students and servants of the Qur'an! You and I are members of a collective personality such as that, worthy of the title of 'perfect man.' We are like the components of a factory's machinery which produces eternal happiness within eternal life. We are hands working on a dominical boat which will disembark the Community of Muhammed (PBUH) at the Realm of Peace, the shore of salvation. So we are surely in need of solidarity and true union, obtained through gaining sincerity -for the mystery of sincerity secures through four individuals the moral strength of one thousand one hundred and eleven- indeed, we are compelled to obtain it.

As also exemplified here, just as how a factory ensures a timely and efficient output only when its machinery works in harmony and does not conflict with itself, so should believers working for a common goal to earn the good pleasure of God exhibit similar harmony. They should strive together without searching for one another's mistakes and defects. In a world where disbelievers ally themselves against the good, are filled with feelings of hatred and envy for the believers, and oppress the poor, the homeless, women, children, and the elderly, all these oppressed people hope for the help of the conscientious. In this case, if wise, sincere, conscientious and honest people use their powers against each other, they may be held accountable for this in the sight of God. It is essential that believers see no limits in improving their alliance, cooperation, friendship, solidarity and affection for another, and never fall into a disagreement which will weaken them. This spirit of believers is best stated in the words of the Prophet Muhammad (pbuh):

You will observe that the believers are like the parts of the body in relation to each other in matters of kindness, love and affection. When one part of the body is afflicted, the entire body feels it; there is loss of sleep and a fever develops.10 The solidarity of the people, who purify themselves of every form of worldly ambition, jealousy and competitiveness, who channel every positive feeling, every effort, and every activity for the good of others, without making it a matter of personal pride, will break the resolve of the alliance of the evil.

Not Valuing The Words of the Evil

The ultimate aim of the evil is to stir up enmity among believers, to wreak their unity and weaken them. As the foregoing makes clear, they are known by their efforts in inventing lies and slandering the good, disgracing them and bringing doubt upon their credibility. However, the stance assumed by the good and conscientious will render such efforts of the slanderers and those committed to evil ineffective. That is because, the existence of people who do not take these slanders seriously, turn a deaf ear to them, and state they do not believe in them, will prevent any harm to the wronged and hinder the evil ones from attaining their mischievous goals.

Indeed, we know that the noble wife of Prophet Muhammad (pbuh) also became the target of such slanderous accusations. God informs us about the kind of attitude the conscientious people should assume when they hear such slander against a believer:

You were bandying it about on your tongues, your mouths uttering something about which you had no knowledge. You

considered it to be a trivial matter, but, in God's sight, it is immense. Why, when you heard it, did you not say, 'We have no business speaking about this. Glory be to You! This is a terrible slander!'? (Surat an-Nur: 15-16)

It is certain that a non-God-fearing person, or someone who has no faith in God, will readily tell lies, concoct slanders, and spread rumours without considering the possible trouble he will inflict on people. That is why, it is unreasonable and wrong to trust people who have no fear in their hearts for God, who have weak religious values, and who thus assume that they will not have to give an account of their deeds in the hereafter. For the same reasons, it is wrong to respond to their accusations without first verifying their validity. In a verse, God explains what the approach of believers should be in such a situation:

You who believe! If a deviator brings you a report, scrutinize it carefully in case you attack people in ignorance and so come to greatly regret what you have done. (Surat al-Hujurat: 6)

An evil-doer is someone who rejects God's commandments. That is the reason why those who are conscientious and just should first investigate the information brought by such people before arriving to a decision.

The Good Only Seek the Good Pleasure of God

That evil, merciless and aggressive people represent the majority, or seem to possess great material wealth, may cause some spiritually weak and ignorant people to develop inaccurate interpretations about them. These people may exaggerate their power and attach more importance to them than they actually deserve. However, the power of people who are distant from God is short-lived and illusory. God is the actual possessor of all the power and resources and it is He who grants such capabilities to people for a time to test them. No man has the power to harm another or to be superior over others merely through his wealth or power. Rather, God grants such potency to test man, though it is all within His grasp.

A man without a strong faith fears cruel people and hesitates to confront them. For this reason, the evil go to great lengths as to please such people and strive to earn their respect. They direct all their talk and behaviour in such a way as to convey the message that they are "on their side", and think that they will earn wealth and power as long as they are under their "wing". Little do they know, however, that such an inclination degrades and dishonours them before God and His sincere servants. It is similar to a man who fears a burglar and thus tries to please him, or someone who tries to behave like a murderer because he is afraid of one.

What is important is to become a person valued by God, the One Who is the Creator and Possessor of everything. For this reason, those who fail to grasp the might of God must be told about the importance of the fear for God and love for Him. They must be told that the evil are actually weak and unable to accomplish anything unless by the Will of God.

In a verse, God informs us of the fact that the good should only have fear for Him and only keep company with those who observe His limits:

You who believe! Have fear of God and be with the truly sincere. (Surat at-Tawba: 119)

The Good Do Not Fear the Censure of Censurers

A devout person only fears God and has a good grasp of the fact that God is the possessor of all power. The only reality these people are concerned with is the Day of Judgement, which they prepare for all their lives. For this reason, it is impossible to threaten such a person with something related to this world, to dishearten them, or to cause them anxiety, fear, hopelessness and pessimism. That is why, the exuberant energy of such a person never abates, no matter what comes upon him in life. Aware that God is his protector, he turns to Him, Who has infinitive mercy, compassion and forgiveness. If he confronts an adversity, a plot, a slander or an unexpected circumstance, he keeps in mind that God is with him, seeing and hearing what the evil are doing. God is the al-Khabir, the one who has knowledge of the most hidden of secrets. That is why, none of those events in life, which would generally be deemed disasters by disbelievers, are intimidating or discouraging to believers. Below are some of the verses in which God mentions people of the past who faced every form of affliction but stood up to them:

> **How many a prophet has fought with many devout man alongside him! They did not give up in the face of what assailed them in the Way of God, nor did they weaken, nor did they yield. God loves the steadfast. All they said was, 'Our Lord, forgive us our wrong actions and any excesses we went to in what we did and make our feet firm and help us against these disbelieving people.' So God gave them the reward of the world and the best reward of the hereafter. God loves good-doers. (Surah Ali 'Imran: 146-148)**

There is another feature to recognise of true believers who are protected and supported by God; they do not fear the censure of any censurers. God conveys this in the answer Prophet Noah (as) gives to his people:

> **Recite to them the story of Noah when he said to his people, 'My people, if my standing here and reminding you of God's Signs has become too much for you to bear, know that I have put my trust in God. So decide, you and your gods, on what you want to do and be open about it. Do with me whatever you decide and do not keep me waiting. (Surah Yunus: 71)**

If one aims to be among the righteous blessed with God's love, favours and the company of His true servants in paradise, then he has to commit himself to remain forthright and honest. Even under the severest threat or unjust treatment, a true believer should not abandon telling and advocating what is true and just. What makes prophets superior is their unyielding insistence in defending the truth, even in hardest of times. Such a resolute and courageous disposition stems from their deep-felt faith. A great example of the

commitment and determination of believers is seen in the answer
the Prophet Shu'ayb (as) gave under threat of death:

> My people! Do as you think best. That is what I am doing. You
> will certainly come to know who will receive a punishment to
> disgrace him, and who is a liar. So look out. I will be on the
> lookout with you.' (Surah Hud: 93)

Just Saying "I Believe" is Enough for a Person to be Considered As a Good Person

One of the attributes of Muslims and the conscientious is that
they do not discriminate between people because of their sex,
culture, social status or any other reason. For instance, one does not
have the right to say "You are not a believer because you fail to do
this..." to someone who clearly maintains that he is a Muslim. No
prejudice is held against a person who says he believes. In any case,
people should always be eager to help when such a person is in need.
God commands in a verse as follows:

> You who believe! When you go out to fight in the Way of God
> verify things carefully. Do not say, 'You are not a believer", to
> someone who greets you as a Muslim, simply out of desire for
> the goods of this world. With God there is booty in abundance.
> That is the way you were before but God has been kind to you.
> So verify things carefully. God is aware of what you do. (Surat
> an-Nisa': 94)

This approach is manifested in the acts of God's Messenger,
Prophet Muhammad (pbuh) in the best way. One hadith that
describes the dialogue between the Prophet Muhammad and a
believer reads:

> I said, 'Messenger of God, say to me something on Islam about which I
> will not ask anyone other than you'. He said, 'Say, "I believe in God"
> then go straight'.

One's faith in God, his closeness to Him and the fear he has for
God is only known by God. Therefore, raising negative charges

against someone who conducts himself like a sincere Muslim and says that he is with the good is utterly prohibited to believers.

The Support of the Good to One Another Should Not be Limited to Words

The majority of people actually have a good grasp of what good, righteous and conscientious conduct is. For this reason, when talking to others, one will find that the majority of people usually accept the good and positive and affirm their commitment to side with the good. However, when it is time to act, most of them remain silent and passive. Although they encounter many situations for which they could side with the good and defend them, they remain ambivalent.

There are many reasons for this silence. Fear of material loss is one of them. For instance, someone defending an innocent person from the alliance of the evil may attract the reaction of the evil and thus, with the fear of some material loss, stop defending him. Accordingly, he may be seized by certain concerns; he may fear that his status, career and reputation may be tarnished, or that he be subjected to slander. Paralysed by fear, they may not say or do what they actually know is just.

However, these people should be aware of the fact that words only please God when they are turned into action. God informs us about people who promise to engage in good deeds but withdraw when it is time to take action:

More fitting for them would be obedience and honourable words. When some matter is resolved, it would be better for them if they acted sincerely towards God. (Surah Muhammad: 21)

For this reason everyone who has faith in God, who is aware that he will give an account of his deeds on the Day of Judgement and, who believes himself to be a sincere and conscientious servant of God, must absolutely ally himself with the good and act with them. God warns people who fail to side with the righteous as follows:

You who believe! Why do you say what you do not do? It is deeply abhorrent to God that you should say what you do not do. (Surat as-Saff: 2-3)

Nobody Should Say "Will My Support Be of Any Help?"

It would be wrong for a person, who witnesses the violence committed against the innocent, recognises the cruelty, mercilessness, immorality, faithlessness around him, and thus feels restless and longs for the establishment of a peaceful and positive environment, to remain passive. Everyone must invest his best effort to spread the moral values of the Qur'an, which is the only way to resolve problems originating from evil, and strive for good and righteousness.

However, Satan certainly aims to gain control over every person who devotes himself to goodness and weaken his resolve. One method Satan employs to discourage a person striving for the good is to make him belittle his efforts and say "What difference would my efforts make?" Faced with all the evil, cruelty, wars and massacres taking place in all corners of the world, a person may feel himself to be feeble and impotent. However, the fact of the matter is quite otherwise. First of all, neither an individual, nor a society, or any other power can bring peace, security, tolerance, love, compassion, friendship and understanding to the world. The One who will establish this blissful environment is our Lord, who has power over all things, who possesses endless might, and who knows what is inside our hearts, and the substance of our thoughts and words.

We, on the other hand, should strive for the good solely as a demonstration of our true and sincere intentions and our service to God, and as a way to earn the rewards of God. A sincere word from someone, a pleasing manner in another, or the patience and commitment one displays, may well set an example for others, make them feel closer to the morality of the Qur'an, and eventually become a propelling force in increasing the number of the good. Ultimately, God will give strength to the good and turn this world into a happy one. Therefore, saying "Would my efforts be of any help?" is only a temptation from Satan, and lending an ear to this temptation is simply a way of avoiding one's responsibility.

As long as one is determined to do what is right and remain conscientious, there are great things that can be accomplished for the cause of good. For example, let us assume that there is a very heavy weight to carry. If only 4 people among 15 commit themselves to carry this weight while the others stand aside because they think "they are too weak to carry the weight", it would not be a wise assertion. However, when 15 of them take on the responsibility and do their best to carry the weight, it would surely lessen the burden of the first 4. What really matters is not "Who does what, to which extent" but to what extent one exerts his own strength.

In a verse of the Qur'an, God informs us that He does "not impose on anyone more than he can stand". For a good person, there is always an easier way of doing things:

Such people are truly racing towards good things, and they are the first to reach them. We do not impose on any self any more than it can stand. With Us there is a Book which speaks the truth. They will not be wronged. (Surat al-Muminun: 61-62)

UNLESS THE GOOD UNITE, CORRUPTION AND CRUELTY WILL PERVADE THE WORLD

In our day, the world is forced to witness unprecedented violence, terror, oppression, fraud, imposture, deceit, immorality, fighting, bickering, poverty and hunger. It is obvious that these evil-inspired happenings are more common in our day than they were in the past days. For this reason, every man of conscience and wisdom needs to avoid all lack of responsibility and become more sensitive towards the suffering and injustice taking place in all parts of the world. The evil are in the majority and appear to be powerful, causing distress and anxiety for many people. Disbelief, or the religion introduced to man which is entirely divorced from the teachings of the original revelations, and non-adherence to the moral values of the Qur'an, have created fertile ground for the proliferation of corruption and all forms of wickedness on earth. God informs man about the devastation brought about by disbelievers to the world as follows:

Among the people there is someone whose words about the

life of the world excite your admiration, and he calls God to witness what is in his heart, while he is in fact the most hostile of adversaries. When he leaves you, he goes about the earth corrupting it, destroying crops and animals. God does not love corruption. (Surat al-Baqara: 204-205)

The way to bring about an end to cruelty and evil of people who have lost all sense of morality and feelings of compassion, who ignore and even ridicule such values, is through the unity of good and conscientious people working for the dissemination of goodness. The kind of environment which will emerge, unless believers cooperate, is stated in the following verse:

Those who disbelieve are the friends and protectors of one another. If you do not act in this way (be friends and protectors of one another) there will be turmoil in the land and great corruption. (Surat al-Anfal: 73)

This is a heavy responsibility upon the believers, each of whom must strictly avoid contributing to such evil consequences. It is time to stop concerning ourselves over self-centred problems and to seriously strive for the good of other people. The majority of people read the stories about prophets and the lives of their companions in details, appreciate and praise the moral perfection they displayed, and talk of their courage and astuteness, their moderate attitude, as well as their resilience which did not bend even under severest hardship. These are the noble and self-sacrificing people God loved and to whom He gave the glad tidings of His paradise as a reward. Throughout their lives, they were unflinchingly honest and righteous. However, in our time, the good should not only talk of these noble people, but also follow in their footsteps. All conscientious people should compete with one another in attaining moral perfection like that of the prophets and the true believers who accompanied them. Otherwise, every conscientious person will be held responsible for all the cruelty, corruption, conflict and wars he witnessed in this world. This point is also stated in many sayings of Our Prophet (pbuh). One of them reads:

If anyone of you sees something objectionable, he should change it with his hand, but if he cannot, he should change it with his tongue, and if he cannot he should do it in his heart, that being the weakest form of faith.

In this century, when the evil have intensified their activities, and the destitute, women and children are in need of so much help, it is essential that Muslims unite and support one another through any adversity, trouble and under other negative circumstances. In Surah Ali 'Imran, God informs us about the sort of brotherhood Muslims should maintain and the attitude a Muslim should adopt toward another Muslim:

Hold fast to the rope of God all together, and do not separate. Remember God's blessing to you when you were enemies and He joined your hearts together so that you became brothers by His blessing. You were on the very brink of a pit of the Fire and He rescued you from it. In this way God makes His Signs clear to you, so that hopefully you will be guided. (Surah Ali 'Imran: 103)

Indifference is Equal to Being a Member of the Alliance of the Evil

As we have discussed earlier, fear of the reactions of the evil may lead to indifference to unjust practises. However, this is not the attitude assumed by people of conscience. This attitude is typical of those who are blindly addicted to this world and who chase after short-lived worldly interests. Those who are hesitant to join the side of the good need to know that their silence and indifference will add to the corruption experienced today all over the world. For instance, if the poor and innocent are massacred in one corner of the world, and the people who claim to be good keep silent and watch it from a distance, they would actually be on the side of the cruel ones. Those who remain silent for fear of the cruelty and possible harm of the evil cannot hope to be rewarded in the hereafter as those who displayed patience.

For example, the people of the Prophet Moses (as) and his brother the prophet Aaron (as) abandoned them to their enemies. Only because of their fear of disbelievers, they became so insensitive that they deserted a man who devoted all his life to the way of God, put his life into jeopardy to save the oppressed, left behind an opulent life in the Pharaoh's palace, strove for the good pleasure of God, and stood bravely against the most cruel man in history. Furthermore, the Prophet Moses (as) and the prophet Aaron (as) were men of courage and faith who resisted all this calamity and hardship only to save their people from the cruelty of the Pharaoh and the torment in hell. The contemptible and cowardly attitude of the people of the Prophet Moses (as) is revealed in the Qur'an as follows:

> Two men among those who were afraid, but whom God had blessed, said, 'Enter the gate against them! Once you have entered it, you will be victorious. Put your trust in God if you are believers.' They said, 'We will never enter it, Moses, as long as they are there. So you and your Lord go and fight. We will stay sitting here.' He said, 'My Lord, I have no control over anyone but myself and my brother, so make a clear distinction between us and this deviant people.' (Surat al-Ma'ida: 23-25)

One point deserves special mention here; the sincere and true believers striving for the way of God receive His support, whether they are alone or not. This is the promise of God to believers. God makes this clear in the following verse:

> If you do not help him, God did help him when the disbelievers drove him out and there were two of them in the cave. He said to his companion, 'Do not be despondent, God is with us.' Then God sent down His serenity upon him and reinforced him with troops you could not see. He made the word of the disbelievers undermost. It is the word of God which is uppermost. God is Almighty, All-Wise. (Surat at-Tawba: 40)

> Before you We sent other Messengers to their people, and they

too brought them the Clear Signs. We took revenge on those who did evil; and it is Our duty to help the believers. (Surat ar-Rum: 47)

This being the case, taking every opportunity to support the alliance of the good with one's best effort is vitally important to attain a blissful afterlife for those who say "I am a conscientious and good person". God's Messenger, the Prophet Muhammad (pbuh), also stated that this will have a reward in the hereafter for a believer:

Whoever removes an anxiety of the world from a believer, God will remove an anxiety on the Day of Resurrection from him. Whoever makes it easy for someone in difficulty, God will make it easy for him in the world and the Next Life.[13]

In the Qur'an, God informs us that those who turn their backs to the good in times of trouble, or do nothing when they are oppressed, will say "Weren't we with you?", when the good will attain felicity and when their rightness will be made clear to everyone:

Those who anticipate the worst for you say, 'Were we not with you?' Whenever you gain a victory from God, but if the disbelievers have a success they say, 'Did we not have the upper hand over you and yet in spite of that keep the believers away from you?' God will judge between you on the Day of Rising. God will not give the disbelievers any way against the believers. (Surat an-Nisa': 141)

In such a circumstance, impartiality would not be an acceptable attitude. On the contrary, as mentioned in the verses above, it is a trait peculiar to hypocrites.

In the face of such cruelty, everyone claiming to be among the good must give all the support they can offer. In this regard, they should first make clear with which party they side. That is because dubious is the sincerity of a person who remains silent about cruelty and fails to lend himself to the oppressed. As stressed numerous times earlier in this book, supporting the evil ones is not necessarily being side by side with them. Remaining indifferent to them serves the very same purpose. God warns man in the Qur'an thus: **"And**

incline not to those who do wrong, or the Fire will seize you." **(Surah Hud: 113)** Being silent is another form of supporting cruelty. In his works, Bediuzzaman Said Nursi describes this situation as follows:

> *The consent given to ignorance is no different than ignorance; the consent given to error, ignorance and cruelty is erroneous, ignorant and cruel.*[14]
>
> *The consent given to oppression is no different than oppression; anyone who sides with the oppressor is an oppressor. Anyone who tends to oppression is subjected to the verse "Do not incline to those who do wrong".*[15]

Therefore, if a man is really a conscientious person, then he should resolutely associate himself with the honest and the good. A contrary attitude would imply being on the side of the evil. If someone does not inform the police about a thief, we cannot call him impartial. This man clearly supports the burglar. Alternatively, watching someone who commits cruelty and turning one's back to evil, saying, "If I try to prevent him, he may also harm me" is simply support of the oppressor. Besides, we must remember that one day one's own house can also be broken by this same thief, or one may be subjected to the same cruelty by the same oppressor. In this sense, the virtuous thing to do is to involve oneself in a concerted effort to prevent the cruelty of such a person even though he does not threaten personal harm. Otherwise, willingly or not, one would be co-operating with the evil. God gives an account of the people on the Day of Judgement who take sides with the good and who take sides with the evil.

Those who perform good actions will receive better than them and will be safe that Day from fear. Those who perform bad actions will be flung head first into the Fire: 'Are you being repaid for anything other than what you did?' (Surat an-Naml: 89-90)

THE PLOTS HATCHED BY THE ALLIANCE OF THE EVIL ARE DOOMED TO FAIL

All through the book we have discussed that the evil has been in an all-out effort to form an alliance against the good. In another section of this book, we stated that the good should act in unity against the ones devising wicked plots. It was further stated that the strength resulting from the unity of the good will ultimately remove all wickedness on earth.

This is what God has promised in the Qur'an. God gives the glad tidings of another fact: the plots and evil plans of the wicked are born to fail no matter how powerful and threatening they might seem. Even within the moment they think they are causing the most distress to believers, they fail to realize that, in the end, it is they themselves will be the ones who will suffer, and receive the greatest harm from their very own plans. However, being unaware of the ultimate end of their plans, they see themselves as victorious. God, who knows the end of all plots even before they were planned, informs us that their plots are doomed to fail:

They concocted their plots, but their plots were with God, even if they were such as to make the mountains vanish. Do not imagine that God will break His promise to His Messengers. God is Almighty, Exactor of Revenge. (Surah Ibrahim: 46-47)

Shown by their arrogance in the land and evil plotting. But evil plotting envelops only those who do it. Do they expect anything but the pattern of previous peoples? You will not find any changing in the pattern of God. You will not find any alteration in the pattern of God. (Surah Fatir: 43)

In another verse, God gives the examples of people from the past and stresses that the evil-doers among them are a defeated group. Just as how the alliance of the evil has always been defeated throughout history, so will the ones living today meet the same end. As a matter of fact, they are defeated from the start:

A defeated host are all the factions that are there! Before them the people of Noah denied the truth, as did 'Ad and Pharaoh of the Stakes, and Thamud and the people of Lut and the Companions of the Thicket. These were the factions. (Surah Sad: 11-13)

God informs us that there is a never-ending and eternal affliction for those who strive for evil in the world, who lead people astray from His path, and who teach them perversity and shamelessness. Before the torment of the hereafter, they will encounter severe affliction also in this world:

Then the final fate of those who did evil will be the worst because they denied God's Signs and mocked at them. (Surat ar-Rum: 10)

Do those who plot evil actions feel secure that God will not cause the earth to swallow them up or that a punishment will not come upon them from where they least expect? (Surat an-Nahl: 45)

Those who associate with the evil alliance, and who value being with the evil for the sake of worldly interests, will regret their choice in the hereafter. They will plead God to severely punish these people they much revered and strictly followed in the world. However their remorse will be futile:

This! A crowd hurtling in with you. There is no welcome for them. They will certainly roast in the Fire. They (who had been

seduced) will say, 'No, it is you who have no welcome. It is you who brought it upon us. What an evil place to settle!' They will say, 'Our Lord, give him who brought this on us double the punishment in the Fire!' (Surah Sad: 59-61)

These cruel people, who present themselves as good and the good as evil ones, will look forward to seeing the good in hell, but to no avail. That is because the good have already taken their places in paradise, the abode of great bliss where they will reside for all eternity as a favour from God.

They will say, 'How is it that we do not see some men whom we used to count among the worst of people? Did we turn them into figures of fun? Did our eyes disdain to look at them?' All this is certainly true - the bickering of the people of the Fire. (Surah Sad: 62-64)

CONCLUSION: ALLIANCE WITH THE GOOD MUST NOT BE DELAYED

The purpose of this book is to make a call the good, conscientious, honest, sincere, optimistic, genial, modest, loyal, faithful, chaste, self-sacrificing, forgiving, agreeable, humble and peaceful people. These wise and sensible people would surely like to hear the exchange of kind words and live in a peaceful and amicable environment where people love and respect one another.

However, we are surrounded by wicked, unscrupulous, pessimistic, insincere, deceiving, selfish, ungrateful, disrespectful, vindictive, unchaste, quarrelsome, bad-tempered, fractious people whose hearts are full of hatred. The number of such people is by no means negligible. Guided by the evil, these people endeavour to spread their wicked ways to all people. Against the alliance of evil, which has become extremely strong and harmful in our day, the good should initiate an all-out resistance, without losing any time groping for the proper conditions, and bothering about what others are saying. In their endeavour, they should be prepared for all the hardship they are likely to face, join forces together with the zeal they derive from their faith, and resist evil with all the power they have.

Today is not the time to look for the mistakes of others or to to look down on others due to their inadequacies. On the contrary, everyone who calls himself a "Muslim" and says "I am a conscientious and good person" should come together and avoid all forms of conduct which would strengthen and encourage the evil.

Postponing the formation of this alliance, or waiting for others to take the initiative, is simply abandoning the oppressed to the cruelty of the evil.

All conscientious people should do their best to live in a world where people approach one another with an amicable and friendly manner, and correct one another's errors with kindness, and where peace, compassion, tolerance, happiness and abundance, in short, where the moral values of the Qur'an pervade. If we conduct ourselves with these principles in mind, our Lord, having infinitive mercy and compassion, will grant us bliss. For this reason, everyone must ally themselves to those who have devoted their entire lives to goodness. We must also remember, that in Surat as-Saff, verse 4, God commands Muslims to be like **"well-built walls."**

THE EVOLUTION MISCONCEPTION

In this book, we have examined nature, plants and the miracle of creation in plants. All these have led us to the conclusion that plants could not have come into being by chance. On the contrary, every detail we have studied in this book points to a superior creation. By contrast, materialism, which seeks to deny the fact of creation in the universe, is nothing but an unscientific fallacy.

Once materialism is invalidated, all other theories based on this philosophy are rendered baseless. Foremost of them is Darwinism, that is, the theory of evolution. This theory, which argues that life originated from inanimate matter through coincidences, has been demolished with the recognition that the universe was created by God. American astrophysicist Hugh Ross explains this as follows:

> *Atheism, Darwinism, and virtually all the "isms" emanating from the eighteenth to the twentieth century philosophies are built upon the assumption, the incorrect assumption, that the universe is infinite. The singularity has brought us face to face with the cause - or causer— beyond/behind/before the universe and all that it contains, including life itself.*[16]

It is God Who created the universe and Who designed it down to its smallest detail. Therefore, it is impossible for the theory of evolution, which holds that living beings are not created by God, but are products of coincidences, to be true.

Unsurprisingly, when we look at the theory of evolution, we see that this theory is denounced by scientific findings. The design in life is extremely complex and striking. In the inanimate world, for instance, we can explore how sensitive are the balances which atoms rest upon, and further, in the animate world, we can observe in what complex designs these atoms were brought together, and how extraordinary are the mechanisms and structures such as proteins, enzymes, and cells, which are manufactured with them.

This extraordinary design in life invalidated Darwinism at the end of the 20th century.

We have dealt with this subject in great detail in some of our other studies, and shall continue to do so. However, we think that, considering its importance, it will be helpful to make a short summary here as well.

The Scientific Collapse of Darwinism

Although a doctrine going back as far as ancient Greece, the theory of evolution was advanced extensively in the 19th century. The most important development that made the theory the top topic of the world of science was the book by Charles Darwin titled The Origin of Species published in 1859. In this book, Darwin denied that different living species on the earth were created separately by God. According to Darwin, all living beings had a common ancestor and they diversified over time through small changes.

Darwin's theory was not based on any concrete scientific finding; as he also accepted, it was just an "assumption." Moreover, as Darwin confessed in the long chapter of his book titled "Difficulties of the Theory," the theory was failing in the face of many critical questions.

Darwin invested all his hopes in new scientific discoveries, which he expected to solve the "Difficulties of the Theory." However, contrary to his expectations, scientific findings expanded the dimensions of these difficulties. The defeat of Darwinism against science can be reviewed under three basic topics:

1) The theory can by no means explain how life originated on the earth.

2) There is no scientific finding showing that the "evolutionary mechanisms" proposed by the theory have any power to evolve at all.

3) The fossil record proves completely the contrary of the suggestions of the theory of evolution.

In this section, we will examine these three basic points in general outlines:

The First Insurmountable Step: The Origin of Life

The theory of evolution posits that all living species evolved from a single living cell that emerged on the primitive earth 3.8 billion years ago. How a single cell could generate millions of complex living species and, if such an evolution really occurred, why traces of it cannot be observed in the fossil record are some of the questions the theory cannot answer. However, first and foremost, of the first step of the alleged evolutionary process it has to be inquired: How did this "first cell" originate?

Since the theory of evolution denies creation and does not accept any kind of supernatural intervention, it maintains that the "first cell" originated coincidentally within the laws of nature, without any design, plan, or arrangement. According to the theory, inanimate matter must have produced a living cell as a result of coincidences. This, however, is a claim inconsistent with even the most unassailable rules of biology.

"Life Comes from Life"

In his book, Darwin never referred to the origin of life. The primitive understanding of science in his time rested on the assumption that living beings had a very simple structure. Since medieval times, spontaneous generation, the theory asserting that non-living materials came together to form living organisms, had been widely accepted. It was commonly believed that insects came into being from food leftovers, and mice from wheat. Interesting experiments were conducted to prove this theory. Some wheat was placed on a dirty piece of cloth, and it was believed that mice would originate from it after a while.

Similarly, worms developing in meat was assumed to be evidence of spontaneous generation. However, only some time later was it understood that worms did not appear on meat spontaneously, but were carried there by flies in the form of larvae, invisible to the naked eye.

Even in the period when Darwin wrote *The Origin of Species*, the belief that bacteria could come into existence from non-living matter was widely accepted in the world of science.

However, five years after Darwin's book was published, the discovery of Louis Pasteur disproved this belief, which constituted the groundwork of evolution. Pasteur summarized the conclusion he reached after time-consuming studies and experiments: *"The claim that inanimate matter can originate life is buried in history for good."*[17]

Advocates of the theory of evolution resisted the findings of Pasteur for a long time. However, as the development of science unraveled the complex structure of the cell of a living being, the idea that life could come into being coincidentally faced an even greater impasse.

Inconclusive Efforts in the 20th Century

The first evolutionist who took up the subject of the origin of life in the 20th century was the renowned Russian biologist Alexander Oparin. With various theses he advanced in the 1930's, he tried to prove that the cell of a living being could originate by coincidence.

These studies, however, were doomed to failure, and Oparin had to make the following confession: "Unfortunately, the origin of the cell remains a question which is actually the darkest point of the entire evolution theory."[18]

Evolutionist followers of Oparin tried to carry out experiments to solve the problem of the origin of life. The best known of these experiments was carried out by American chemist Stanley Miller in 1953. Combining the gases he alleged to have existed in the primordial earth's atmosphere in an experiment set-up, and adding energy to the mixture, Miller synthesized several organic molecules (amino acids) present in the structure of proteins.

Barely a few years had passed before it was revealed that this experiment, which was then presented as an important step in the name of evolution, was invalid, the atmosphere used in the experiment having been very different from real earth conditions.[19]

After a long silence, Miller confessed that the atmosphere medium he used was unrealistic.[20]

All the evolutionist efforts put forth throughout the 20th century to explain the origin of life ended with failure. The geochemist Jeffrey Bada from San Diego Scripps Institute accepts this fact in an article published in Earth Magazine in 1998:

Today as we leave the twentieth century, we still face the biggest unsolved problem that we had when we entered the twentieth century: How did life originate on Earth?[21]

The Complex Structure of Life

The primary reason why the theory of evolution ended up in such a big impasse about the origin of life is that even the living organisms deemed the simplest have incredibly complex structures. The cell of a living being is more complex than all of the technological products produced by man. Today, even in the most developed laboratories of the world, a living cell cannot be produced by bringing inorganic materials together.

The conditions required for the formation of a cell are too great in quantity to be explained away by coincidences. The probability of proteins, the building blocks of cell, being synthesized coincidentally, is 1 in 10950 for an average protein made up of 500 amino acids. In mathematics, a probability smaller than 1 over 1050 is practically considered to be impossible.

The DNA molecule, which is located in the nucleus of the cell and which stores genetic information, is an incredible databank. It is calculated that if the information coded in DNA were written down, this would make a giant library consisting of 900 volumes of encyclopaedias of 500 pages each.

A very interesting dilemma emerges at this point: the DNA can only replicate with the help of some specialized proteins (enzymes). However, the synthesis of these enzymes can only be realized by the information coded in DNA. As they both depend on each other, they have to exist at the same time for replication. This brings the scenario that life originated by itself to a deadlock. Prof. Leslie Orgel, an evolutionist of repute from the University of San Diego, California, confesses this fact in the September 1994 issue of the *Scientific American* magazine:

> *It is extremely improbable that proteins and nucleic acids, both of which are structurally complex, arose spontaneously in the same place at the same time. Yet it also seems impossible to have one without the other. And so, at first glance, one might have to conclude that life could never, in fact, have originated by chemical means.*

No doubt, if it is impossible for life to have originated from natural causes, then it has to be accepted that life was "created" in a supernatural way. This fact explicitly invalidates the theory of evolution, whose main purpose is to deny creation.

Imaginary Mechanisms of Evolution

The second important point that negates Darwin's theory is that both concepts put forward by the theory as "evolutionary mechanisms" were understood to have, in reality, no evolutionary power.

Darwin based his evolution allegation entirely on the mechanism of "natural selection". The importance he placed on this mechanism was evident in the name of his book: *The Origin of Species, By Means Of Natural Selection...*

Natural selection holds that those living things that are stronger and more suited to the natural conditions of their habitats will survive in the struggle for life. For example, in a deer herd under the threat of attack by wild animals, those that can run faster will survive. Therefore, the deer herd will be comprised of faster and stronger individuals. However, unquestionably, this mechanism will not cause deer to evolve and transform themselves into another living species, for instance, horses.

Therefore, the mechanism of natural selection has no evolutionary power. Darwin was also aware of this fact and had to state this in his book The Origin of Species:

> *Natural selection can do nothing until favourable variations chance to occur.*[23]

Lamarck's Impact

So, how could these "favourable variations" occur? Darwin tried to answer this question from the standpoint of the primitive understanding of science in his age. According to the French biologist Lamarck, who lived before Darwin, living creatures passed on the traits they acquired during their lifetime to the next generation and these traits, accumulating from one generation to another, caused new species to be formed. For instance, according to Lamarck, giraffes evolved from antelopes; as they struggled to eat the leaves of high trees, their necks were extended from generation to generation.

Darwin also gave similar examples, and in his book *The Origin of Species*, for instance, said that some bears going into water to find food transformed themselves into whales over time.[24]

However, the laws of inheritance discovered by Mendel and verified by the science of genetics that flourished in the 20th century, utterly demolished the legend that acquired traits were passed on to subsequent generations. Thus, natural selection fell out of favour as an evolutionary mechanism.

Neo-Darwinism and Mutations

In order to find a solution, Darwinists advanced the "Modern Synthetic Theory", or as it is more commonly known, Neo-Darwinism, at the end of the 1930's. Neo-Darwinism added mutations, which are distortions formed in the genes of living beings because of external factors such as radiation or replication errors, as the "cause of favourable variations" in addition to natural mutation.

Today, the model that stands for evolution in the world is Neo-Darwinism. The theory maintains that millions of living beings present on the earth formed as a result of a process whereby numerous complex organs of these organisms such as the ears, eyes, lungs, and wings, underwent "mutations," that is, genetic disorders. Yet, there is an outright scientific fact that totally undermines this theory: Mutations do not cause living beings to develop; on the contrary, they always cause harm to them.

The reason for this is very simple: the DNA has a very complex structure and random effects can only cause harm to it. American geneticist B.G. Ranganathan explains this as follows:

Mutations are small, random, and harmful. They rarely occur and the best possibility is that they will be ineffectual. These four characteristics of mutations imply that mutations cannot lead to an evolutionary development. A random change in a highly specialised organism is either ineffectual or harmful. A random change in a watch cannot improve the watch. It will most probably harm it or at best be ineffectual. An earthquake does not improve the city, it brings destruction. [25]

Not surprisingly, no mutation example, which is useful, that is, which is observed to develop the genetic code, has been observed so far. All mutations have proved to be harmful. It was understood that mutation, which is presented as an "evolutionary mechanism," is actually a genetic occurrence that harms living beings, and leaves them disabled. (The most common effect of mutation on human beings is cancer). No doubt, a destructive mechanism cannot be an "evolutionary mechanism." Natural selection, on the other hand, "can do nothing by itself" as Darwin also accepted. This fact shows us that there is no "evolutionary mechanism" in nature. Since no evolutionary mechanism exists, neither could any imaginary process called evolution have taken place.

The Fossil Record: No Sign of Intermediate Forms

The clearest evidence that the scenario suggested by the theory of evolution did not take place is the fossil record.

According to the theory of evolution, every living species has sprung from a predecessor. A previously existing species turned into something else in time and all species have come into being in this way. According to the theory, this transformation proceeds gradually over millions of years.

Had this been the case, then numerous intermediary species should have existed and lived within this long transformation period.

For instance, some half-fish/half-reptiles should have lived in the past which had acquired some reptilian traits in addition to the fish traits they already had. Or there should have existed some reptile-birds, which acquired some bird traits in addition to the reptilian traits they already had. Since these would be in a transitional phase, they should be disabled, defective, crippled living beings. Evolutionists refer to these imaginary creatures, which they believe to have lived in the past, as "transitional forms."

If such animals had really existed, there should be millions and even billions of them in number and variety. More importantly, the remains of these strange creatures should be present in the fossil record. In The Origin of Species, Darwin explained:

If my theory be true, numberless intermediate varieties, linking most closely all of the species of the same group together must assuredly have existed... Consequently, evidence of their former existence could be found only amongst fossil remains.[26]

Darwin's Hopes Shattered

However, although evolutionists have been making strenuous efforts to find fossils since the middle of the 19th century all over the world, no transitional forms have yet been uncovered. All the fossils unearthed in excavations showed that, contrary to the expectations of evolutionists, life appeared on earth all of a sudden and fully-formed.

A famous British paleontologist, Derek V. Ager, admits this fact, even though he is an evolutionist:

The point emerges that if we examine the fossil record in detail, whether at the level of orders or of species, we find - over and over again - not gradual evolution, but the sudden explosion of one group at the expense of another.[27]

This means that in the fossil record, all living species suddenly emerge as fully formed, without any intermediate forms in between. This is just the opposite of Darwin's assumptions. Also, it is very strong evidence that living beings are created. The only explanation of a living species emerging suddenly and complete in every detail without any evolutionary ancestor can be that this species was created. This fact is admitted also by the widely known evolutionist biologist Douglas Futuyma:

Creation and evolution, between them, exhaust the possible explanations for the origin of living things. Organisms either appeared on the earth fully developed or they did not. If they did not, they must have developed from pre-existing species by some process of modification. If they did appear in a fully developed state, they must indeed have been created by some omnipotent intelligence.[28]

Fossils show that living beings emerged fully developed and in a perfect state on the earth. That means that "the origin of species" is, contrary to Darwin's supposition, not evolution but creation.

The Tale of Human Evolution

The subject most often brought up by the advocates of the theory of evolution is the subject of the origin of man. The Darwinist claim holds that the modern men of today evolved from some kind of ape-like creatures. During this alleged evolutionary process, which is supposed to have started 4-5 million years ago, it is claimed that there existed some "transitional forms" between modern man and his ancestors. According to this completely imaginary scenario, four basic "categories" are listed:

1. Australopithecus
2. Homo habilis
3. Homo erectus
4. Homo sapiens

Evolutionists call the so-called first ape-like ancestors of men "Australopithecus" which means "South African ape." These living beings are actually nothing but an old ape species that has become extinct. Extensive research done on various Australopithecus specimens by two world famous anatomists from England and the USA, namely, Lord Solly Zuckerman and Prof. Charles Oxnard, has shown that these belonged to an ordinary ape species that became extinct and bore no resemblance to humans.[29]

Evolutionists classify the next stage of human evolution as "homo," that is "man." According to the evolutionist claim, the living beings in the Homo series are more developed than Australopithecus. Evolutionists devise a fanciful evolution scheme by arranging different fossils of these creatures in a particular order. This scheme is imaginary because it has never been proved that there is an evolutionary relation between these different classes. Ernst Mayr, one of the foremost defenders of the theory of evolution in the 20th century, admits this fact by saying that "the chain reaching as far as Homo sapiens is actually lost."[30]

By outlining the link chain as "Australopithecus > Homo habilis > Homo erectus > Homo sapiens," evolutionists imply that each of these species is one another's ancestor. However, recent findings of paleoanthropologists have revealed that Australopithecus, Homo habilis and Homo erectus lived at different parts of the world at the same time.[31]

Moreover, a certain segment of humans classified as Homo erectus have lived up until very modern times. Homo sapiens neandarthalensis and Homo sapiens sapiens (modern man) co-existed in the same region.[32]

This situation apparently indicates the invalidity of the claim that they are ancestors of one another. A paleontologist from Harvard University, Stephen Jay Gould, explains this deadlock of the theory of evolution although he is an evolutionist himself:

What has become of our ladder if there are three coexisting lineages of hominids (A. africanus, the robust australopithecines, and H. habilis), none clearly derived from another? Moreover, none of the three display any evolutionary trends during their tenure on earth.[33]

Put briefly, the scenario of human evolution, which is sought to be upheld with the help of various drawings of some "half ape, half human" creatures appearing in the media and course books, that is, frankly, by means of propaganda, is nothing but a tale with no scientific ground.

Lord Solly Zuckerman, one of the most famous and respected scientists in the U.K., who carried out research on this subject for years, and particularly studied Australopithecus fossils for 15 years, finally concluded, despite being an evolutionist himself, that there is, in fact, no such family tree branching out from ape-like creatures to man.

Zuckerman also made an interesting "spectrum of science." He formed a spectrum of sciences ranging from those he considered scientific to those he considered unscientific. According to

Zuckerman's spectrum, the most "scientific"–that is, depending on concrete data–fields of science are chemistry and physics. After them come the biological sciences and then the social sciences. At the far end of the spectrum, which is the part considered to be most "unscientific," are "extra-sensory perception"–concepts such as telepathy and sixth sense–and finally "human evolution." Zuckerman explains his reasoning:

We then move right off the register of objective truth into those fields of presumed biological science, like extrasensory perception or the interpretation of man's fossil history, where to the faithful (evolutionist) anything is possible - and where the ardent believer (in evolution) is sometimes able to believe several contradictory things at the same time.

The tale of human evolution boils down to nothing but the prejudiced interpretations of some fossils unearthed by certain people, who blindly adhere to their theory.

Technology In The Eye and The Ear

Another subject that remains unanswered by evolutionary theory is the excellent quality of perception in the eye and the ear.

Before passing on to the subject of the eye, let us briefly answer the question of "how we see". Light rays coming from an object fall oppositely on the retina of the eye. Here, these light rays are transmitted into electric signals by cells and they reach a tiny spot at the back of the brain called the centre of vision. These electric signals are perceived in this centre of the brain as an image after a series of processes. With this technical background, let us do some thinking.

The brain is insulated from light. That means that the inside of the brain is solid dark, and light does not reach the location where the brain is situated. The place called the centre of vision is a solid dark place where no light ever reaches; it may even be the darkest place you have ever known. However, you observe a luminous, bright world in this pitch darkness.

The image formed in the eye is so sharp and distinct that even the technology of the 20th century has not been able to attain it. For instance, look at the book you read, your hands with which you hold it, then lift your head and look around you. Have you ever seen such a sharp and distinct image as this one at any other place? Even the most developed television screen produced by the greatest television producer in the world cannot provide such a sharp image for you. This is a three-dimensional, coloured, and extremely sharp image. For more than 100 years, thousands of engineers have been trying to achieve this sharpness. Factories, huge premises were established, much research has been done, plans and designs have been made for this purpose. Again, look at a TV screen and the book you hold in your hands. You will see that there is a big difference in sharpness and distinction. Moreover, the TV screen shows you a two-dimensional image, whereas with your eyes, you watch a three-dimensional perspective having depth.

For many years, ten of thousands of engineers have tried to make a three-dimensional TV, and reach the vision quality of the eye. Yes, they have made a three-dimensional television system but it is not possible to watch it without putting on glasses; moreover, it is only an artificial three-dimension. The background is more blurred, the foreground appears like a paper setting. Never has it been possible to produce a sharp and distinct vision like that of the eye. In both the camera and the television, there is a loss of image quality.

Evolutionists claim that the mechanism producing this sharp and distinct image has been formed by chance. Now, if somebody told you that the television in your room was formed as a result of chance, that all its atoms just happened to come together and make up this device that produces an image, what would you think? How can atoms do what thousands of people cannot?

If a device producing a more primitive image than the eye could not have been formed by chance, then it is very evident that the eye and the image seen by the eye could not have been formed by chance. The same situation applies to the ear. The outer ear picks up the available sounds by the auricle and directs them to the middle ear; the middle ear transmits the sound vibrations by intensifying them; the inner ear sends these vibrations to the brain by translating them into electric signals. Just as with the eye, the act of hearing finalises in the centre of hearing in the brain.

The situation in the eye is also true for the ear. That is, the brain is insulated from sound just like it is from light: it does not let any sound in. Therefore, no matter how noisy is the outside, the inside of the brain is completely silent. Nevertheless, the sharpest sounds are perceived in the brain. In your brain, which is insulated from sound, you listen to the symphonies of an orchestra, and hear all the noises in a crowded place. However, if the sound level in your brain was measured by a precise device at that moment, it would be seen that a complete silence is prevailing there.

As is the case with imagery, decades of effort have been spent in trying to generate and reproduce sound that is faithful to the original. The results of these efforts are sound recorders, high-fidelity systems, and systems for sensing sound. Despite all this technology and the thousands of engineers and experts who have been working on this endeavour, no sound has yet been obtained that has the same sharpness and clarity as the sound perceived by the ear. Think of the highest-quality HI-FI systems produced by the biggest company in the music industry. Even in these devices, when sound is recorded some of it is lost; or when you turn on a HI-FI you always hear a hissing sound before the music starts. However, the sounds that are the products of the technology of the human body are extremely sharp and clear. A human ear never perceives a sound accompanied by a hissing sound or with atmospherics as does HI-FI; it perceives sound exactly as it is, sharp and clear. This is the way it has been since the creation of man.

So far, no visual or recording apparatus produced by man has been as sensitive and successful in perceiving sensory data as are the eye and the ear.

However, as far as seeing and hearing are concerned, a far greater fact lies beyond all this.

To Whom Does the Consciousness that Sees and Hears Within the Brain Belong?

Who is it that watches an alluring world in its brain, listens to symphonies and the twittering of birds, and smells the rose? The stimulations coming from the eyes, ears, and nose of a human being travel to the brain as electro-chemical nervous impulses. In biology, physiology, and biochemistry books, you can find many details about how this image forms in the brain. However, you will never come across the most important fact about this subject: Who is it that perceives these electro-chemical nervous impulses as images, sounds, odours and sensory events in the brain? There is a consciousness in the brain that perceives all this without feeling any need for eye, ear, and nose. To whom does this consciousness belong? There is no doubt that this consciousness does not belong to the nerves, the fat layer and neurons comprising the brain. This is why Darwinist-materialists, who believe that everything is comprised of matter, cannot give any answer to these questions.

For this consciousness is the spirit created by God. The spirit needs neither the eye to watch the images, nor the ear to hear the sounds. Furthermore, nor does it need the brain to think.

Everyone who reads this explicit and scientific fact should ponder on Almighty God, should fear Him and seek refuge in Him, He Who squeezes the entire universe in a pitch-dark place of a few cubic centimeters in a three-dimensional, coloured, shadowy, and luminous form.

A Materialist Faith

The information we have presented so far shows us that the theory of evolution is a claim evidently at variance with scientific findings. The theory's claim on the origin of life is inconsistent with science, the evolutionary mechanisms it proposes have no evolutionary power, and fossils demonstrate that the intermediate forms required by the theory never existed. So, it certainly follows that the theory of evolution should be pushed aside as an unscientific idea. This is how many ideas such as the earth-centered universe model have been taken out of the agenda of science throughout history.

However, the theory of evolution is pressingly kept on the agenda of science. Some people even try to represent criticisms directed against the theory as an "attack on science." Why?

The reason is that the theory of evolution is an indispensable dogmatic belief for some circles. These circles are blindly devoted to materialist philosophy and adopt Darwinism because it is the only materialist explanation that can be put forward for the workings of nature.

Interestingly enough, they also confess this fact from time to time. A well known geneticist and an outspoken evolutionist, Richard C. Lewontin from Harvard University, confesses that he is "first and foremost a materialist and then a scientist":

> It is not that the methods and institutions of science somehow compel us accept a material explanation of the phenomenal world, but, on the contrary, that we are forced by our a priori adherence to material causes to create an apparatus of investigation and a set of concepts that produce material explanations, no matter how counter-intuitive, no matter how mystifying to the uninitiated. Moreover, that materialism is absolute, so we cannot allow a Divine Foot in the door.[35]

These are explicit statements that Darwinism is a dogma kept alive just for the sake of adherence to the materialist philosophy. This dogma maintains that there is no being save matter. Therefore, it argues that inanimate, unconscious matter created life. It insists that millions of different living species; for instance, birds, fish, giraffes, tigers, insects, trees, flowers, whales and human beings originated as a result of the interactions between matter such as the pouring rain, the lightning flash, etc., out of inanimate matter. This is a precept contrary both to reason and science. Yet Darwinists continue to defend it just so as "not to allow a Divine Foot in the door."

Anyone who does not look at the origin of living beings with a materialist prejudice will see this evident truth: All living beings are works of a Creator, Who is All-Powerful, All-Wise and All-Knowing. This Creator is God, Who created

---

They said 'Glory be to You!
We have no knowledge except what You have taught us.
You are the All-Knowing, the All-Wise.'
(Surat al-Baqarah: 32)

NOTES

1. Imam an-Nawawi, *The Complete Forty Hadith*, p. 5

2. Tirmidhi, *Sayings of Muhammad* by Prof. Ghazi Ahmad

3. *Sayings of Muhammad* by Prof. Ghazi Ahmad

4. Bukhari, Muslim, *Hayaat-ul-Muslimeen*, by Mohammad Ashraf Ali Thanvi

5. Hadith of Abu Dawud, On the Authority of Abu Hurayrah, *Words of the Prophet Muhammad* by Maulana Wahiduddin Khan, p. 54

6. Hadith of Al-Bukhari and Muslim, *Words of the Prophet Muhammad*, p. 67

7. Imam an-Nawawi, *The Complete Forty Hadith*, p. 122

8. Bediuzzaman Said Nursi, *Risale-i Nur Külliyati II* (The Risale-i Nur Collection II), The Flashes Collection, The Twentieth Flash

9. Bediuzzaman Said Nursi, *Risale-i Nur Külliyati II* (The Risale-i Nur Collection II), The Flashes Collection, The Twenty-first Flash

10. Hadith of Al-Bukhari and Muslim on the Authority of Nu'man Ibn Bashir, Words *of the Prophet* Muhammad by Maulana Wahiduddin Khan, p. 68

11. Imam an-Nawawi, *The Complete Forty Hadith*, p. 85

12. Muslim, *Sayings of Muhammad*, by Prof. Ghazi Ahmad

13. Imam an-Nawawi, *The Complete Forty Hadith*, p. 125

14. Bediuzzaman Said Nursi, *Risale-i Nur Külliyati II* (The Risale-i Nur Collection II), Emirdag Lahikasi (Emirdag Letters), Nesil Yayinlari, page 1183

15. Bediuzzaman Said Nursi, *Risale-i Nur Külliyati II* (The Risale-i Nur Collection II), Kastamonu Lahikasi (Kastamonu Letters), p. 158

16. Hugh Ross, *The Fingerprint of God*, p. 50

17. Sidney Fox, Klaus Dose. *Molecular Evolution and The Origin of Life*, New York: Marcel Dekker, 1977. p. 2

18. Alexander I. Oparin, *Origin of Life*, (1936) New York, Dover Publications, 1953 (Reprint), p. 196

19. *"New Evidence on Evolution of Early Atmosphere and Life"*, Bulletin of the American Meteorological Society, Vol. 63, November 1982, p. 1328-1330.

20. Stanley Miller, *Molecular Evolution of Life: Current Status of the Prebiotic Synthesis of Small Molecules*, 1986, p. 7

21. Jeffrey Bada, Earth, February 1998, p. 40

22. Leslie E. Orgel, "The Origin of Life on Earth", *Scientific American*, Vol 271, October 1994, p. 78

23. Charles Darwin, *The Origin of Species: A Facsimile of the First Edition*, Harvard University Press, 1964, p. 189

24. Charles Darwin, *The Origin of Species: A Facsimile of the First Edition*, Harvard University Press, 1964, p. 184.

25. B. G. Ranganathan, *Origins?*, Pennsylvania: The Banner Of Truth Trust, 1988.

26. Charles Darwin, *The Origin of Species: A Facsimile of the First Edition*, Harvard University Press, 1964, p. 179

27. Derek A. Ager, *"The Nature of the Fossil Record"*, Proceedings of the British Geological Association, Vol. 87, 1976, p. 133

28. Douglas J. Futuyma, *Science on Trial*, New York: Pantheon Books, 1983. p. 197

29. Solly Zuckerman, *Beyond The Ivory Tower, New York:* Toplinger Publications, 1970, pp. 75-94; Charles E. Oxnard, *"The Place of Australopithecines in Human Evolution: Grounds for Doubt"*, Nature, Vol. 258, p. 389

30. J. Rennie, "Darwin's Current Bulldog: Ernst Mayr", *Scientific American*, December 1992

31. Alan Walker, *Science*, vol. 207, 1980, s. 1103; A. J. Kelso, *Physical Antropology, 1st ed.*, New York: J. B. Lipincott Co., 1970, p. 221; M. D. Leakey, Olduvai Gorge, vol. 3, Cambridge: Cambridge University Press, 1971, p. 272

32. *Time*, November 1996

33. S. J. Gould, *Natural History*, vol. 85, 1976, p. 30

34. Solly Zuckerman, Beyond The *Ivory Tower,*. New York: Toplinger Publications, 1970, p. 19

35. Richard Lewontin, *"The Demon-Haunted World",* The New York Review of Books, 9 January, 1997, p. 28

Also by Harun Yahya

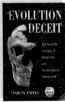   

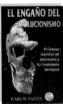    

Many people think that Darwin's Theory of Evolution is a proven fact. Contrary to this conventional wisdom, recent developments in science completely disprove the theory. The only reason Darwinism is still foisted on people by means of a worldwide propaganda campaign lies in the ideological aspects of the theory. All secular ideologies and philosophies try to provide a basis for themselves by relying on the theory of evolution.

This book clarifies the scientific collapse of the theory of evolution in a way that is detailed but easy to understand. It reveals the frauds and distortions committed by evolutionists to "prove" evolution. Finally it analyzes the powers and motives that strive to keep this theory alive and make people believe in it.

Anyone who wants to learn about the origin of living things, including mankind, needs to read this book. *The Evolution Deceit* is also available in Italian, Albanian, Spanish, Indonesian, Russian and Serbo-Croat (Bosnian).

"Everything that constitutes our life is a totality of perceptions received by our soul. The things, people, places and events that make our world and our lives meaningful are like a dream; we perceive them only as images in our brain, and have nothing to do with their truth or reality..."

In the book, which consists of a conversation between four people, the prejudices that prevent people from understanding this great truth are removed, and the misconceptions they have are explained.

When a person examines his own body or any other living thing in nature, the world or the whole universe, in it he sees a great design, art, plan and intelligence. All this is evidence proving God's being, unit, and eternal power.

For Men of Understanding was written to make the reader see and realise some of the evidence of creation in nature. For Men of Understanding is also available in Indonesian, German and Russian.

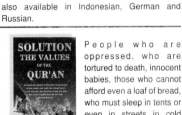

People who are oppressed, who are tortured to death, innocent babies, those who cannot afford even a loaf of bread, who must sleep in tents or even in streets in cold weather, those who are massacred just because they belong to a certain tribe, women, children, and old people who are expelled from their homes because of their religion...Eventually, there is only one solution to the injustice, chaos, terror, massacres, hunger, poverty, and oppression: the morals of the Qur'an.

How was matter and time created from nothingness? What does the Big Bang theory signify about the creation of the universe? What is the parallelism between Einstein's Theory of Relativity and the Qur'anic verses?

All of these questions are answered in this book. If you want to learn the truths about space, matter, time and fate, read this book.

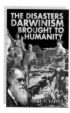 

Fascism and communism, which made humanity suffer dark times, are considered to be opposed ideas. However, these ideologies are fed from the same source, on the grounds of which they can attract masses to their side. This source has never drawn attention, always remaining behind the scenes. This source is the materialist philosophy and its adaptation to nature, which is DARWINISM. The acknowledgement of the scientific invalidity of this theory that serves as a basis for cruel dictators and vicious ideological trends will bring about the end of all these detrimental ideologies. This book is also available in French.

Never plead ignorance of God's evident existence, that everything was created by God, that everything you own was given to you by God for your subsistence, that you will not stay so long in this world, of the reality of death, that the Qur'an is the Book of truth, that you will give account for your deeds, of the voice of your conscience that always invites you to righteousness, of the existence of the hereafter and the day of account, that hell is the eternal home of severe punishment, and of the reality of fate.

Darwin's theory of evolution maintained that all living beings emerged as a result of chance coincidence and thus denied Creation. Yet, scientific developments did not favour the evolutionist standpoint and simply opposed it. Different branches of science like biochemistry, genetics, and palaeontology have demonstrated that the claims that life originated as a result of "coincidences" is foolish. This is a book you will read with pleasure and as it makes explicitly clear why the theory of evolution is the greatest aberration in the history of science.

People who are oppressed, who are tortured to death, innocent babies, those who cannot afford even a loaf of bread, who must sleep in tents or even in streets in cold weather, those who are massacred just because they belong to a certain tribe, women, children, and old people who are expelled from their homes because of their religion... Eventually, there is only one solution to the injustice, chaos, terror, massacres, hunger, poverty, and oppression: the morals of the Qur'an.

Colours, patterns, spots even lines of each living being existing in nature have a meaning. An attentive eye would immediately recognise that not only the living beings, but also everything in nature are just as they should be. Furthermore, he would realise that everything is given to the service of man: the comforting blue colour of the sky, the colourful view of flowers, the bright green trees and meadows, the moon and stars illuminating the world in pitch darkness together with innumerable beauties surrounding man *Allah's Artistry in Colour* is also available in Arabic.

The unprecedented style and the superior wisdom inherent in the Qur'an is conclusive evidence confirming that it is the Word of God. Apart from this, there are a number of miracles verifying the fact that the Qur'an is the revelation of God, one of them being that, 1,400 years ago, it declared a number of scientific facts that have only been established thanks to the technological breakthroughs of the 20th century. In this book, in addition to the scientific miracles of the Qur'an, you will also find messages regarding the future. *Miracles of the Qur'an* is also available in Serbo-Croat (Bosnian).

Man is a being to which God has granted the faculty of thinking. Yet a majority of people fail to employ this faculty as they should...The purpose of this book is to summon people to think in the way they should and to guide them in their efforts to think. This book is also available in Indonesian.

These millimeter-sized animals that we frequently come across but don't care much about have an excellent ability for organization and specialization that is not to be matched by any other being on earth. These aspects of ants create in one a great admiration for God's superior power and unmatched creation.

Today, science has proven that the universe was created from nothing with a Big Bang. Moreover, all physical balances of the universe are designed to support human life. Everything from the nuclear reactions in stars to the chemical properties of a carbon atom or a water molecule, is created in a glorious harmony. This is the exalted and flawless creation of God, the Lord of All the Worlds. *The Creation of the Universe* is also available in French.

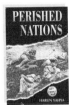 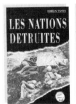

Many societies that rebelled against the will of God or regarded His messengers as enemies were wiped off the face of the earth completely... *Perished Nations* examines these penalties as revealed in the verses of the Quran and in light of archaeological discoveries. This book is also available in German, French, Spanish, Russian and Portuguese.

The way to examine the universe and all the beings therein and to discover God's art of creation and announce it to humanity is "science". Therefore, religion adopts science as a way to reach the details of God's creation and therefore encourages science. Just as religion encourages scientific research, so does scientific research that is guided by the facts communicated by religion yield very repid and definite results. This is because religion is the unique source that provides the most correct and definite answer to the question of how the universe and life came into being.

In this book you will find explanations about eternity, timelessness and spacelessness that you will never have encountered anywhere else and you will be confronted by the reality that eternity has already begun. The real answers to many questions people always ponder such as the true nature of death, resurrection after death, the existence of an eternal life, and the time when all these things will happen are to be found here...

We fall sick many times throughout our lives. When the events of "sickness" and "recovering" take place, our bodies become a battleground in which a bitter struggle is taking place. Microbes invisible to our eyes intrude into our body and begin to increase rapidly. The body however has a mechanism that combats them. Known as the "immune system", this mechanism is the most disciplined, most complex and successful army of the world. This system proves that the human body is the outcome of a unique design that has been planned with a great wisdom and skill. In other words, the human body is the evidence of a flawless creation, which is the peerless creation of God.

In a body that is made up of atoms, you breathe in air, eat food, and drink liquids that are all composed of atoms. Everything you see is nothing but the result of the collision of electrons of atoms with photons.
In this book, the implausibility of the spontaneous formation of an atom, the building-block of everything, living or non-living, is related and the flawless nature of God's creation is demonstrated.

There are questions about religion that people seek answers to and hope to be enlightened in the best way. However in most cases, people base their opinions on hearsay rather than acquiring them from the real source of religion: the Qur'an. In these booklets, you will find the most accurate answers to all the questions you seek answers for and learn your responsibilities towards your Creator.

This book deals with how the theory of evolution is invalidated by scientific findings and experiments in a concise and simple language.

Scientific progress makes it clear that living beings have an extremely complex structure and an order that is too perfect to have come into being by accident. Recently, for example, the perfect structure in the human gene became a top issue as a result of hte completion of the Human Genome Project. In this book, the unique creation of God is once again disclosed for all to see.

Just as a tiny key opens a huge door, this book will open new horizons for its readers. And the reality behind that door is the most important reality that one can come across in one's lifetime. Relating the amazing and admirable features of spiders known by few people and asking the questions of "how" and "why" in the process, this book reveals the excellence and perfection inherent in God's creation.

In the Qur'an, conscience has a meaning and importance beyond its common and everyday use. This book introduces the real concept of conscience that is related in the Qur'an and draws our attention to the kind of understanding, thought, and wisdom that a truly conscientious person has.

God, in the Qur'an, calls the culture of people who are not subject to the religion of God "ignorance." Only a comparison of this culture with the honourable thoughts and moral structure of the Qur'an can reveal its primitive and corrupted nature. The purpose of this book is to take this comparison further, displaying the extent of the "crude understanding" of ignorant societies.

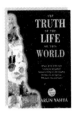

The world is a temporary place specially created by God to test man. That is why, it is inherently flawed and far from satisfying man's endless needs and desires. Each and every attraction existing in the world eventually wears out, becomes corrupt, decays and finally disappears. This is the never-changing reality of life. This book explains this most important essence of life and leads man to ponder the real place to which he belongs, namely the Hereafter.

In the Qur'an, there is an explicit reference to the "second coming of the Jesus to the world" which is heralded in a hadith. The realisation of some information revealed in the Qur'an about Jesus can only be possible by Jesus' second coming...

In the Qur'an, God tells people many secrets. People who are unaware of these secrets experience the trouble and distress caused by this throughout their lives. For those who learn these secrets of the Qur'an, however, the life of this world is very easy, and full of joy and excitement. This book deals with the subjects God related to people as a secret.

The Qur'an has been sent down as a book easily understandable to everyone. Everyone who believes in God and follows his conscience can take counsel from the verses of the Qur'an and obey the commands in the verses. However, those who follow their lower self fail to measure God with His true scale, entertain doubts about the hereafter, interpret the verses of the Qur'an wrongly in their own crooked reasoning. In this book, the reasons why those who do not use their intellect misinterpret the Qur'an are examined and some examples of the unwise interpretations and objections they make concerning the verses are reviewed and answered.

The plan, design, and delicate balance existing in our bodies and reaching into even the remotest corners of the incredibly vast universe must surely have a superior Creator. Man is unable to see his Creator yet he can nevertheless grasp His existence, strength, and wisdom by means of his intellect. This book is a summons to think. A summons to ponder over the universe and living beings and see how they have been created flawlessly.

One of the principal deceptions that impels people into delinquency and makes them pursue their own desires is their heedlessness of death. Both human beings and the universe they live in are mortal. What awaits the disbelievers in the next world is more dreadful: the eternal wrath of hell. This book, based on the verses of the Qur'an, makes a detailed depiction of the moment of death, the day of judgement, and the penalties in hell, and it sounds a warning about the great danger facing us. *Death Resurrection* Hell is also available in Polish.

The purpose of this book is to warn people against the day on which they will say "If only we did not rebel against God. If only we listened to the messengers..." and therefore feel deep regret. This is a summons to live for the cause of God when there is still time. *Before You Regret* is also available in French.

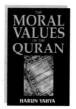

A study that examines and seeks to remind us of the basic moral principles of the Qur'an, particularly those that are most likely to be forgotten or neglected at times.

The Qur'an has been revealed to us so that we may read and ponder. The Basic Concepts of the Qur'an is a useful resource prepared as a guide to thinking. Some basic Islamic concepts like the soul, conscience, wisdom, loyalty, submission to God, brotherhood, modesty, prayer, patience, are discussed in the light of Qur'anic verses. This book is also available in Portuguese.

Children!
Have you ever asked yourself questions like these: How did our earth come into existence? How did the moon and sun come into being? Where were you before you were born? How did oceans, trees, animals appear on earth? How does a little tiny bee know how to produce delicious honey? How can it build a honeycomb with such astonishingly regular edges? Who was the first human being? In this book you will find the true answers to these questions.

The most serious mistake a man makes is not pondering. It is not possible to find the truth unless one thinks about basic questions such as "How and why am I here?", "Who created me?", or "Where am I going?." Failing to do so, one becomes trapped in the vicious circle of daily life and turns into a selfish creature caring only for himself. Ever Thought About the Truth? summons people to think on such basic questions and to discover the real meaning of life. This book is also available in French.

Children's Books

These books, prepared for kids, are about the miraculous characteristics of the living things on the Earth. Full colour and written in a concise style, these books give your children the opportunity to get to know God and His perfect artistry in creation. The World of Our Little Friends: The Ants is also available in Russian and French. Honeybees that Build Perfect Combs is also available in French.